The Smart Camper Journal & Logbook

The Essential RV, Tent Camping, Glamping, and Boondocking Logbook, Planner & Journal

Special Planning Sections for Meals, Maintenance & Supplies

By

Ron Samson

Published by:

CSBA Publishing

CSBA Publishing House

Cover & Interior designed

By

Jessica Freeman

First Edition

Contents

How to Use this Guide

Thank you for purchasing this journal! I hope that the entries in it help you to recall the good (and maybe not so good) moments on your camping travels.

Whether you're tent camping, van boondocking, RV camping, glamping, or just tagging along, this logbook will help you to chronicle and keep track of your experiences.

There are enough log pages to catalog 50 campground stays. In the back of the book, you'll find 4 extra sections to help you organize your trip – maintenance logs, a supply list, weekly menu planner, and a quick reference system for finding your log entries.

Use the log sheets to record as much or as little information about each campground as you'd like. Don't forget to rate each campground online, wherever you find your most reliable ratings.

You'll notice that each listing has a log number at the top. When you complete a log entry, just record the page number, log number, and campground name in the quick reference section. Each state has its own table. The quick reference guide is listed in tables alphabetically by state.

The maintenance logs will help you to keep track of what routine work, upgrades, or problem issues you addressed with regards to your RV. You can note the date, what was done, and who did the service in this section.

A prepared camper is a happy camper!

The supply lists are categorized by date and trip. There is a checklist of common needs for every RV trip along with room to list your own supplies that you need to pack.

When you're traveling via camper, eating healthy can be a real challenge. The menu planner section will help you with figuring out what food supplies to pack for your trip. It is categorized in tables by date, then leaves you room to plan breakfasts, lunches, dinners, and snacks by day of the week.

Consider using a different logbook for each year – or even each season – depending on how often you travel.

I hope this book helps you recall the good moments and helps you steer clear of those places where you might not have enjoyed yourself quite as much.

The open road is a wondrous place! Happy trails!

If found, please return to

(Name)

_____

(Address)

_____

_____

(Phone) _____

Part 1: Log Sheets

Log # 1

Stop #_____ **in State**

_____

Campground: _____

Traveling Companions:

Site #

How Reservation Was Made:
        Online   Phone

Who recommended this place?

Reservation #

Reservation Notes:
(Who took it, who made it, how far in advance?)

Date Arrived:

Day of the Week:

Time Arrived:

Address:

Zip Code:

Website:

Travelled From:

Preferred Route:

Date Departed:

Day of the Week:

Time Departed:

State:

Telephone:

GPS:

Mileage:

Routes to Avoid:

Sites Along the Way:

What Type of Campground?
   National Forest State Park Private
   Army Corps of Engineers County
     Beurue of Land Mgmt Other

Rate:

Deposit Amount:

Types of hookups:
      Electric ___ Amps ____
  Sewer _____ Dump Station ___

Security Attendant: Yes No
When?_____

Rate Notes: (Discounts, extra fees?)

Water Hookups?

Pressure Notes:

Gate Code:

Amenities

Showers: Hot Water   Pay Shower
Dry Area   Other _____

Restroom notes:

Pool   Hot Tub   Lodge Room
Game Room

Adult Center   Restaurant
Shuffleboard

Pickleball   Tennis   Mini Golf

Fishing   Gym/Fitness Center

Other Amenities:

Things to Do

What to do while there:

What to do nearby:

Restaurants:

Wildlife we saw:

Nearby campgrounds to consider:

Grocery/General stores nearby:

Pets allowed?

Cell phone service: YES   NO

How many bars of service, usually?

Was the Wi-Fi fast/reliable?

Allow tents?

Scenery:

Weather:

Roads: Paved   Gravel   Dirt

Site Size: Small Medium Large

Parking notes:

Overall Noise Rating: Quiet Light
Road Noise Loud   Train Noises
Loud Road Noise

Ratings: Google _____ Yelp _____ Trip Advisor _____ Campendium _____ Good Sam _____

Our personal rating: ★ ★ ★ ★ ★

A good memory:

A not-so-good memory:

Log # 2

**Stop
#_____
in
State**

_____

Campground:
_____

Traveling Companions:

Site #

How Reservation Was Made:
　　　　　Online　　Phone

Who recommended this place?

Reservation #

Reservation Notes:
(Who took it, who made it, how far in advance?)

Date Arrived:

Day of the Week:

Time Arrived:

Address:

Zip Code:

Website:

Travelled From:

Preferred Route:

Date Departed:

Day of the Week:

Time Departed:

State:

Telephone:

GPS:

Mileage:

Routes to Avoid:

Sites Along the Way:

What Type of Campground?
　　National Forest　State Park　Private
　　　Army Corps of Engineers　County
　　　　Beurue of Land Mgmt　Other

Rate:

Deposit Amount:

Types of hookups:
　　　　Electric ___ Amps ____
　　Sewer _____ Dump Station ___

Security Attendant: Yes　No
When?_____

Rate Notes: (Discounts, extra fees?)

Water Hookups?

Pressure Notes:

Gate Code:

Amenities

Showers: Hot Water   Pay Shower
Dry Area   Other _____

    Pool   Hot Tub   Lodge Room
        Game Room

    Pickleball   Tennis   Mini Golf

Other Amenities:

Restroom notes:

    Adult Center   Restaurant
        Shuffleboard

Fishing   Gym/Fitness Center

Things to Do

What to do while there:

What to do nearby:

Restaurants:

Wildlife we saw:

Nearby campgrounds to consider:

Grocery/General stores nearby:

Pets allowed?

Cell phone service: YES   NO

How many bars of service, usually?

Was the Wi-Fi fast/reliable?

Allow tents?

Scenery:

Weather:

Roads: Paved   Gravel   Dirt

Site Size: Small Medium Large

Parking notes:

Overall Noise Rating: Quiet Light
Road Noise Loud   Train Noises
Loud Road Noise

Ratings: Google ____   Yelp ____ Trip Advisor ____   Campendium ____   Good Sam ____

Our personal rating: ★ ★ ★ ★ ★

A good memory:

A not-so-good memory:

Log # 3

Stop #_____
in
State

_____

Campground: _____

Traveling Companions:

Site #

How Reservation Was Made:
         Online   Phone

Who recommended this place?

Reservation #

Reservation Notes:
(Who took it, who made it, how far in advance?)

Date Arrived:

Day of the Week:

Time Arrived:

Address:

Zip Code:

Website:

Travelled From:

Preferred Route:

Date Departed:

Day of the Week:

Time Departed:

State:

Telephone:

GPS:

Mileage:

Routes to Avoid:

Sites Along the Way:

Rate:

Deposit Amount:

Types of hookups:
      Electric ___ Amps ___
   Sewer _____ Dump Station ___

Security Attendant: Yes No
When?_____

What Type of Campground?
   National Forest State Park Private
    Army Corps of Engineers County
      Beurue of Land Mgmt Other

Rate Notes: (Discounts, extra fees?)

Water Hookups?

Pressure Notes:

Gate Code:

Amenities

Showers: Hot Water   Pay Shower
Dry Area   Other _____

Restroom notes:

Pool   Hot Tub   Lodge Room
Game Room

Adult Center   Restaurant
Shuffleboard

Pickleball   Tennis   Mini Golf

Fishing   Gym/Fitness Center

Other Amenities:

Things to Do

What to do while there:

What to do nearby:

Restaurants:

Wildlife we saw:

Nearby campgrounds to consider:

Grocery/General stores nearby:

Pets allowed?

Cell phone service: YES   NO

How many bars of service, usually?

Was the Wi-Fi fast/reliable?

Allow tents?

Scenery:

Weather:

Roads: Paved   Gravel   Dirt

Site Size: Small Medium Large

Parking notes:

Overall Noise Rating: Quiet Light
Road Noise Loud   Train Noises
Loud Road Noise

Ratings: Google _____ Yelp _____ Trip Advisor _____ Campendium _____ Good Sam _____

Our personal rating: ★ ★ ★ ★ ★

A good memory:

A not-so-good memory:

Log # 4

Stop #_____
in
State

_____

Campground:

Traveling Companions:

Site #

How Reservation Was Made:
      Online   Phone

Who recommended this place?

Reservation #

Reservation Notes:
(Who took it, who made it, how far in advance?)

Date Arrived:
Day of the Week:
Time Arrived:
Address:
Zip Code:
Website:
Travelled From:
Preferred Route:

Date Departed:
Day of the Week:
Time Departed:
State:
Telephone:
GPS:
Mileage:
Routes to Avoid:

Sites Along the Way:

What Type of Campground?
  National Forest State Park Private
  Army Corps of Engineers County
  Beurue of Land Mgmt Other

Rate:
Deposit Amount:
Types of hookups:
    Electric ____ Amps ____
  Sewer _____ Dump Station ____

Security Attendant: Yes No
When?_____

Rate Notes: (Discounts, extra fees?)

Water Hookups?
Pressure Notes:

Gate Code:

Amenities

Showers: Hot Water   Pay Shower
Dry Area   Other _____

Restroom notes:

Pool   Hot Tub   Lodge Room
Game Room

Adult Center   Restaurant
Shuffleboard

Pickleball   Tennis   Mini Golf

Fishing   Gym/Fitness Center

Other Amenities:

Things to Do

What to do while there:

What to do nearby:

Restaurants:

Wildlife we saw:

Nearby campgrounds to consider:

Grocery/General stores nearby:

Pets allowed?

Cell phone service: YES   NO

How many bars of service, usually?

Was the Wi-Fi fast/reliable?

Allow tents?

Scenery:

Weather:

Roads: Paved   Gravel   Dirt

Site Size: Small Medium Large

Parking notes:

Overall Noise Rating: Quiet Light
Road Noise Loud   Train Noises
Loud Road Noise

Ratings: Google ____ Yelp ____ Trip Advisor _____ Campendium _____ Good Sam _____

Our personal rating: ★ ★ ★ ★ ★

A good memory:

A not-so-good memory:

Log # 5

Stop #_____ in State
_____

Campground:
_____

Traveling Companions:

Site #   Reservation #

How Reservation Was Made: Reservation Notes:
        Online   Phone   (Who took it, who made it, how far in
Who recommended this place?   advance?)

Date Arrived: Date Departed:

Day of the Week: Day of the Week:

Time Arrived: Time Departed:

Address: State:

Zip Code: Telephone:

Website: GPS:

Travelled From: Mileage:

Preferred Route: Routes to Avoid:

Sites Along the Way: What Type of Campground?
                                              National Forest   State Park   Private
                                              Army Corps of Engineers   County
                                                  Beurue of Land Mgmt   Other

Rate: Rate Notes: (Discounts, extra fees?)

Deposit Amount:

Types of hookups: Water Hookups?
        Electric ___ Amps ____   Pressure Notes:
    Sewer _____ Dump Station ___

Security Attendant: Yes   No   Gate Code:
When?_____

Amenities

Showers: Hot Water   Pay Shower
Dry Area   Other _____

Restroom notes:

    Pool   Hot Tub   Lodge Room
            Game Room

    Adult Center   Restaurant
          Shuffleboard

    Pickleball   Tennis   Mini Golf

Fishing   Gym/Fitness Center

Other Amenities:

Things to Do

What to do while there:

What to do nearby:

Restaurants:

Wildlife we saw:

Nearby campgrounds to consider:

Grocery/General stores nearby:

Pets allowed?

Cell phone service: YES   NO

How many bars of service, usually?

Was the Wi-Fi fast/reliable?

Allow tents?

Scenery:

Weather:

Roads: Paved   Gravel   Dirt

Site Size: Small Medium Large

Parking notes:

Overall Noise Rating: Quiet Light
Road Noise Loud   Train Noises
Loud Road Noise

Ratings: Google _____ Yelp _____ Trip Advisor _____ Campendium _____ Good Sam _____

Our personal rating: ☆ ☆ ☆ ☆ ☆

A good memory:

A not-so-good memory:

Log # 6

Stop #_____ in State

_____

Traveling Companions:

Site #

How Reservation Was Made:
　　　Online　Phone

Who recommended this place?

Reservation #

Reservation Notes:
(Who took it, who made it, how far in advance?)

Date Arrived:

Day of the Week:

Time Arrived:

Address:

Zip Code:

Website:

Travelled From:

Preferred Route:

Date Departed:

Day of the Week:

Time Departed:

State:

Telephone:

GPS:

Mileage:

Routes to Avoid:

Sites Along the Way:

What Type of Campground?
　　National Forest　State Park　Private
　　Army Corps of Engineers　County
　　　Beurue of Land Mgmt　Other

Rate:

Deposit Amount:

Types of hookups:
　　　Electric ___ Amps ____
　　Sewer _____ Dump Station ___

Security Attendant: Yes　No
When?_____

Rate Notes: (Discounts, extra fees?)

Water Hookups?

Pressure Notes:

Gate Code:

Amenities

Showers: Hot Water   Pay Shower   Dry Area   Other _____

Restroom notes:

Pool   Hot Tub   Lodge Room   Game Room

Adult Center   Restaurant   Shuffleboard

Pickleball   Tennis   Mini Golf

Fishing   Gym/Fitness Center

Other Amenities:

Things to Do

What to do while there:

What to do nearby:

Restaurants:

Wildlife we saw:

Nearby campgrounds to consider:

Grocery/General stores nearby:

Pets allowed?

Cell phone service: YES   NO

How many bars of service, usually?

Was the Wi-Fi fast/reliable?

Allow tents?

Scenery:

Weather:

Roads: Paved   Gravel   Dirt

Site Size: Small Medium Large

Parking notes:

Overall Noise Rating: Quiet Light Road Noise Loud Train Noises Loud Road Noise

Ratings: Google _____   Yelp _____ Trip Advisor _____ Campendium _____ Good Sam _____

Our personal rating: ⭐ ⭐ ⭐ ⭐ ⭐

A good memory:

A not-so-good memory:

Log # 7

Stop #_____ **in State**
_____

Campground:

Traveling Companions:

Site #

How Reservation Was Made:
    Online   Phone

Who recommended this place?

Reservation #

Reservation Notes:
(Who took it, who made it, how far in advance?)

Date Arrived:

Day of the Week:

Time Arrived:

Address:

Zip Code:

Website:

Travelled From:

Preferred Route:

Date Departed:

Day of the Week:

Time Departed:

State:

Telephone:

GPS:

Mileage:

Routes to Avoid:

Sites Along the Way:

What Type of Campground?
    National Forest   State Park   Private
    Army Corps of Engineers   County
    Beurue of Land Mgmt   Other

Rate:

Deposit Amount:

Types of hookups:
    Electric ___ Amps ____
    Sewer _____ Dump Station ___

Security Attendant: Yes   No
When?_____

Rate Notes: (Discounts, extra fees?)

Water Hookups?

Pressure Notes:

Gate Code:

Showers: Hot Water   Pay Shower
Dry Area   Other _____

Restroom notes:

Pool   Hot Tub   Lodge Room
Game Room

Adult Center   Restaurant
Shuffleboard

Pickleball   Tennis   Mini Golf

Fishing   Gym/Fitness Center

Other Amenities:

Things to Do

What to do while there:

What to do nearby:

Restaurants:

Wildlife we saw:

Nearby campgrounds to consider:

Grocery/General stores nearby:

Pets allowed?

Cell phone service: YES   NO

How many bars of service, usually?

Was the Wi-Fi fast/reliable?

Allow tents?

Scenery:

Weather:

Roads: Paved   Gravel   Dirt

Site Size: Small Medium Large

Parking notes:

Overall Noise Rating: Quiet Light
Road Noise Loud   Train Noises
Loud Road Noise

Ratings: Google _____ Yelp _____ Trip Advisor _____ Campendium _____ Good Sam _____

Our personal rating: ★ ★ ★ ★ ★

A good memory:

A not-so-good memory:

Log # 8

**Stop
#_____
in
State**

_____

Campground:

Traveling Companions:

Site #

Reservation #

How Reservation Was Made:

Online   Phone

Who recommended this place?

Reservation Notes:

(Who took it, who made it, how far in advance?)

Date Arrived:

Day of the Week:

Time Arrived:

Address:

Zip Code:

Website:

Travelled From:

Preferred Route:

Date Departed:

Day of the Week:

Time Departed:

State:

Telephone:

GPS:

Mileage:

Routes to Avoid:

Sites Along the Way:

What Type of Campground?

National Forest   State Park   Private
Army Corps of Engineers   County
Beurue of Land Mgmt   Other

Rate:

Deposit Amount:

Types of hookups:

Electric ___ Amps ___
Sewer ___ Dump Station ___

Security Attendant: Yes   No
When?_____

Rate Notes: (Discounts, extra fees?)

Water Hookups?

Pressure Notes:

Gate Code:

Amenities

Showers: Hot Water   Pay Shower
Dry Area   Other _____

Restroom notes:

Pool   Hot Tub   Lodge Room
Game Room

Adult Center   Restaurant
Shuffleboard

Pickleball   Tennis   Mini Golf

Fishing   Gym/Fitness Center

Other Amenities:

Things to Do

What to do while there:

What to do nearby:

Restaurants:

Wildlife we saw:

Nearby campgrounds to consider:

Grocery/General stores nearby:

Pets allowed?

Cell phone service: YES   NO

How many bars of service, usually?

Was the Wi-Fi fast/reliable?

Allow tents?

Scenery:

Weather:

Roads: Paved   Gravel   Dirt

Site Size: Small Medium Large

Parking notes:

Overall Noise Rating: Quiet Light
Road Noise Loud   Train Noises
Loud Road Noise

Ratings: Google _____ Yelp _____ Trip Advisor _____ Campendium _____ Good Sam _____

Our personal rating: ★ ★ ★ ★ ★

A good memory:

A not-so-good memory:

Log # 9

Stop #_____
in
State

_____

Campground:

Traveling Companions:

Site #

How Reservation Was Made:
        Online   Phone

Who recommended this place?

Reservation #

Reservation Notes:
(Who took it, who made it, how far in advance?)

Date Arrived:

Day of the Week:

Time Arrived:

Address:

Zip Code:

Website:

Travelled From:

Preferred Route:

Date Departed:

Day of the Week:

Time Departed:

State:

Telephone:

GPS:

Mileage:

Routes to Avoid:

Sites Along the Way:

What Type of Campground?
   National Forest   State Park   Private
   Army Corps of Engineers   County
      Beurue of Land Mgmt   Other

Rate:

Deposit Amount:

Types of hookups:
        Electric ___ Amps ____
    Sewer _____ Dump Station ___

Security Attendant: Yes   No
When?_____

Rate Notes: (Discounts, extra fees?)

Water Hookups?

Pressure Notes:

Gate Code:

Amenities

Showers: Hot Water   Pay Shower
Dry Area   Other _____

     Pool   Hot Tub   Lodge Room
         Game Room

     Pickleball   Tennis   Mini Golf

Other Amenities:

Restroom notes:

     Adult Center   Restaurant
         Shuffleboard

Fishing   Gym/Fitness Center

Things to Do

What to do while there:

What to do nearby:

Restaurants:

Wildlife we saw:

Nearby campgrounds to consider:

Grocery/General stores nearby:

Pets allowed?

Cell phone service: YES   NO

How many bars of service, usually?

Was the Wi-Fi fast/reliable?

Allow tents?

Scenery:

Weather:

Roads: Paved   Gravel   Dirt

Site Size: Small   Medium   Large

Parking notes:

Overall Noise Rating: Quiet Light
Road Noise Loud   Train Noises
Loud Road Noise

Ratings: Google _____ Yelp _____ Trip Advisor _____ Campendium _____ Good Sam _____

Our personal rating: ★ ★ ★ ★ ★

A good memory:

A not-so-good memory:

Log # 10

Stop
#_____
in
State

_____

Campground: _____

Traveling Companions: _____

Site # _____   Reservation # _____

How Reservation Was Made: Reservation Notes:

       Online   Phone   (Who took it, who made it, how far in advance?)

Who recommended this place?

Date Arrived: Date Departed:

Day of the Week: Day of the Week:

Time Arrived: Time Departed:

Address: State:

Zip Code: Telephone:

Website: GPS:

Travelled From: Mileage:

Preferred Route: Routes to Avoid:

Sites Along the Way: What Type of Campground?

     National Forest   State Park   Private

     Army Corps of Engineers   County

     Beurue of Land Mgmt   Other

Rate: Rate Notes: (Discounts, extra fees?)

Deposit Amount:

Types of hookups: Water Hookups?

     Electric ____ Amps ____   Pressure Notes:

     Sewer _____ Dump Station ____

Security Attendant: Yes   No   Gate Code:

When?_____

Amenities

Showers: Hot Water   Pay Shower   Dry Area   Other _____

Restroom notes:

Pool   Hot Tub   Lodge Room
Game Room

Adult Center   Restaurant
Shuffleboard

Pickleball   Tennis   Mini Golf

Fishing   Gym/Fitness Center

Other Amenities:

Things to Do

What to do while there:

What to do nearby:

Restaurants:

Wildlife we saw:

Nearby campgrounds to consider:

Grocery/General stores nearby:

Pets allowed?

Cell phone service: YES   NO

How many bars of service, usually?

Was the Wi-Fi fast/reliable?

Allow tents?

Scenery:

Weather:

Roads: Paved   Gravel   Dirt

Site Size: Small Medium Large

Parking notes:

Overall Noise Rating: Quiet Light
Road Noise Loud Train Noises
Loud Road Noise

Ratings: Google _____ Yelp _____ Trip Advisor _____ Campendium _____ Good Sam _____

Our personal rating: ★ ★ ★ ★ ★

A good memory:

A not-so-good memory:

Log # 11

Stop #_____
in
State

_____

Campground: _____

Traveling Companions:

Site #

How Reservation Was Made:

        Online   Phone

Who recommended this place?

Reservation #

Reservation Notes:

(Who took it, who made it, how far in advance?)

Date Arrived:

Day of the Week:

Time Arrived:

Address:

Zip Code:

Website:

Travelled From:

Preferred Route:

Date Departed:

Day of the Week:

Time Departed:

State:

Telephone:

GPS:

Mileage:

Routes to Avoid:

Sites Along the Way:

What Type of Campground?

   National Forest State Park Private

    Army Corps of Engineers County

      Beurue of Land Mgmt Other

Rate:

Deposit Amount:

Types of hookups:

      Electric ____ Amps ____

   Sewer _____ Dump Station ____

Security Attendant: Yes No
When?_____

Rate Notes: (Discounts, extra fees?)

Water Hookups?

Pressure Notes:

Gate Code:

Amenities

Showers: Hot Water   Pay Shower
Dry Area   Other _____

Restroom notes:

    Pool   Hot Tub   Lodge Room
        Game Room

    Adult Center   Restaurant
        Shuffleboard

    Pickleball   Tennis   Mini Golf

Fishing   Gym/Fitness Center

Other Amenities:

Things to Do

What to do while there:

What to do nearby:

Restaurants:

Wildlife we saw:

Nearby campgrounds to consider:

Grocery/General stores nearby:

Pets allowed?

Cell phone service: YES   NO

How many bars of service, usually?

Was the Wi-Fi fast/reliable?

Allow tents?

Scenery:

Weather:

Roads: Paved   Gravel   Dirt

Site Size: Small Medium Large

Parking notes:

Overall Noise Rating: Quiet Light
Road Noise Loud   Train Noises
Loud Road Noise

Ratings: Google _____ Yelp _____ Trip Advisor _____ Campendium _____ Good Sam _____

Our personal rating: ★ ★ ★ ★ ★

A good memory:

A not-so-good memory:

Log # 12

Stop #_____
in
State

_____

Campground: _____

Traveling Companions: _____

Site # _____   Reservation # _____

How Reservation Was Made: Reservation Notes:
       Online   Phone   (Who took it, who made it, how far in
Who recommended this place?   advance?)

Date Arrived: Date Departed:
Day of the Week: Day of the Week:
Time Arrived: Time Departed:
Address: State:
Zip Code: Telephone:
Website: GPS:
Travelled From: Mileage:
Preferred Route: Routes to Avoid:

Sites Along the Way: What Type of Campground?
                                    National Forest State Park Private
                                    Army Corps of Engineers County
                                    Beurue of Land Mgmt Other

Rate: Rate Notes: (Discounts, extra fees?)
Deposit Amount:
Types of hookups: Water Hookups?
      Electric ____ Amps ____   Pressure Notes:
   Sewer _____ Dump Station ____

Security Attendant: Yes No   Gate Code:
When?_____

Amenities

Showers: Hot Water   Pay Shower   Dry Area   Other _____

Restroom notes:

Pool   Hot Tub   Lodge Room   Game Room

Pickleball   Tennis   Mini Golf

Adult Center   Restaurant   Shuffleboard

Fishing   Gym/Fitness Center

Other Amenities:

Things to Do

What to do while there:

What to do nearby:

Restaurants:

Wildlife we saw:

Nearby campgrounds to consider:

Grocery/General stores nearby:

Pets allowed?

Cell phone service: YES   NO

How many bars of service, usually?

Was the Wi-Fi fast/reliable?

Allow tents?

Scenery:

Weather:

Roads: Paved   Gravel   Dirt

Site Size: Small Medium Large

Parking notes:

Overall Noise Rating: Quiet Light Road Noise Loud   Train Noises Loud Road Noise

Ratings: Google _____ Yelp _____ Trip Advisor _____ Campendium _____ Good Sam _____

Our personal rating: ★ ★ ★ ★ ★

A good memory:

A not-so-good memory:

Log # 13

**Stop
#_____
in
State**

_____

Traveling Companions:

Site #

How Reservation Was Made:
        Online   Phone

Who recommended this place?

Reservation #

Reservation Notes:
(Who took it, who made it, how far in advance?)

Date Arrived:

Day of the Week:

Time Arrived:

Address:

Zip Code:

Website:

Travelled From:

Preferred Route:

Date Departed:

Day of the Week:

Time Departed:

State:

Telephone:

GPS:

Mileage:

Routes to Avoid:

Sites Along the Way:

What Type of Campground?
    National Forest   State Park   Private
    Army Corps of Engineers   County
        Beurue of Land Mgmt   Other

Rate:

Deposit Amount:

Types of hookups:
        Electric ___ Amps ____
    Sewer _____ Dump Station ___

Security Attendant: Yes   No
When?_____

Rate Notes: (Discounts, extra fees?)

Water Hookups?

Pressure Notes:

Gate Code:

Showers: Hot Water   Pay Shower
Dry Area   Other _____

Restroom notes:

        Pool   Hot Tub   Lodge Room
               Game Room

        Adult Center   Restaurant
                Shuffleboard

        Pickleball   Tennis   Mini Golf

        Fishing   Gym/Fitness Center

Other Amenities:

Things to Do

What to do while there:

What to do nearby:

Restaurants:

Wildlife we saw:

Nearby campgrounds to consider:

Grocery/General stores nearby:

Pets allowed?

Cell phone service: YES   NO

How many bars of service, usually?

Was the Wi-Fi fast/reliable?

Allow tents?

Scenery:

Weather:

Roads: Paved   Gravel   Dirt

Site Size: Small Medium Large

Parking notes:

Overall Noise Rating: Quiet Light
Road Noise Loud   Train Noises
Loud Road Noise

Ratings: Google _____ Yelp _____ Trip Advisor _____ Campendium _____ Good Sam _____

Our personal rating: ★ ★ ★ ★ ★

A good memory:

A not-so-good memory:

Log # 14

Stop #_____
in
State

_____

Campground:

Traveling Companions:

Site #

How Reservation Was Made:
            Online   Phone

Who recommended this place?

Reservation #

Reservation Notes:
(Who took it, who made it, how far in advance?)

Date Arrived:

Day of the Week:

Time Arrived:

Address:

Zip Code:

Website:

Travelled From:

Preferred Route:

Date Departed:

Day of the Week:

Time Departed:

State:

Telephone:

GPS:

Mileage:

Routes to Avoid:

Sites Along the Way:

What Type of Campground?
    National Forest   State Park   Private
        Army Corps of Engineers   County
            Beurue of Land Mgmt   Other

Rate:

Deposit Amount:

Types of hookups:
        Electric ___ Amps ____
    Sewer _____ Dump Station ___

Security Attendant: Yes   No
When?_____

Rate Notes: (Discounts, extra fees?)

Water Hookups?

Pressure Notes:

Gate Code:

Amenities

Showers: Hot Water Pay Shower
Dry Area Other _____

Restroom notes:

    Pool Hot Tub Lodge Room
        Game Room

    Adult Center Restaurant
        Shuffleboard

    Pickleball Tennis Mini Golf

Fishing Gym/Fitness Center

Other Amenities:

Things to Do

What to do while there:

What to do nearby:

Restaurants:

Wildlife we saw:

Nearby campgrounds to consider:

Grocery/General stores nearby:

Pets allowed?

Cell phone service: YES   NO

How many bars of service, usually?

Was the Wi-Fi fast/reliable?

Allow tents?

Scenery:

Weather:

Roads: Paved Gravel   Dirt

Site Size: Small Medium Large

Parking notes:

Overall Noise Rating: Quiet Light
Road Noise Loud Train Noises
Loud Road Noise

Ratings: Google _____ Yelp _____ Trip Advisor _____ Campendium _____ Good Sam _____

Our personal rating: ★ ★ ★ ★ ★

A good memory:

A not-so-good memory:

Log # 15

Stop #_____
in
State

_____

Campground:

Traveling Companions:

Site #

How Reservation Was Made:
         Online   Phone

Who recommended this place?

Reservation #

Reservation Notes:
(Who took it, who made it, how far in advance?)

Date Arrived:

Day of the Week:

Time Arrived:

Address:

Zip Code:

Website:

Travelled From:

Preferred Route:

Date Departed:

Day of the Week:

Time Departed:

State:

Telephone:

GPS:

Mileage:

Routes to Avoid:

Sites Along the Way:

What Type of Campground?
   National Forest   State Park   Private
   Army Corps of Engineers   County
      Beurue of Land Mgmt   Other

Rate:

Deposit Amount:

Types of hookups:
      Electric ___ Amps ____
   Sewer _____ Dump Station ___

Security Attendant: Yes   No
When?_____

Rate Notes: (Discounts, extra fees?)

Water Hookups?

Pressure Notes:

Gate Code:

Amenities

Showers: Hot Water   Pay Shower
Dry Area   Other _____

Restroom notes:

Pool   Hot Tub   Lodge Room
Game Room

Adult Center   Restaurant
Shuffleboard

Pickleball   Tennis   Mini Golf

Fishing   Gym/Fitness Center

Other Amenities:

Things to Do

What to do while there:

What to do nearby:

Restaurants:

Wildlife we saw:

Nearby campgrounds to consider:

Grocery/General stores nearby:

Pets allowed?

Cell phone service: YES   NO

How many bars of service, usually?

Was the Wi-Fi fast/reliable?

Allow tents?

Scenery:

Weather:

Roads: Paved   Gravel   Dirt

Site Size: Small Medium Large

Parking notes:

Overall Noise Rating: Quiet Light
Road Noise Loud   Train Noises
Loud Road Noise

Ratings: Google _____ Yelp _____ Trip Advisor _____ Campendium _____ Good Sam _____

Our personal rating: ★ ★ ★ ★ ★

A good memory:

A not-so-good memory:

Log # 16

Stop
#_____
in
State

_____

Campground: _____

Traveling Companions:

Site #   Reservation #

How Reservation Was Made: Reservation Notes:
        Online   Phone   (Who took it, who made it, how far in
Who recommended this place?   advance?)

Date Arrived: Date Departed:

Day of the Week: Day of the Week:

Time Arrived: Time Departed:

Address: State:

Zip Code: Telephone:

Website: GPS:

Travelled From: Mileage:

Preferred Route: Routes to Avoid:

Sites Along the Way: What Type of Campground?
                            National Forest   State Park   Private
                            Army Corps of Engineers   County
                            Beurue of Land Mgmt   Other

Rate: Rate Notes: (Discounts, extra fees?)

Deposit Amount:

Types of hookups: Water Hookups?
        Electric ___ Amps ____   Pressure Notes:
     Sewer _____ Dump Station ___

Security Attendant: Yes   No   Gate Code:
When?_____

Amenities

Showers: Hot Water   Pay Shower   Dry Area   Other _____

Restroom notes:

Pool   Hot Tub   Lodge Room   Game Room

Adult Center   Restaurant   Shuffleboard

Pickleball   Tennis   Mini Golf

Fishing   Gym/Fitness Center

Other Amenities:

Things to Do

What to do while there:

What to do nearby:

Restaurants:

Wildlife we saw:

Nearby campgrounds to consider:

Grocery/General stores nearby:

Pets allowed?

Cell phone service: YES   NO

How many bars of service, usually?

Was the Wi-Fi fast/reliable?

Allow tents?

Scenery:

Weather:

Roads: Paved   Gravel   Dirt

Site Size: Small Medium Large

Parking notes:

Overall Noise Rating: Quiet Light Road Noise Loud   Train Noises Loud Road Noise

Ratings: Google _____ Yelp _____ Trip Advisor _____ Campendium _____ Good Sam _____

Our personal rating: ★ ★ ★ ★ ★

A good memory:

A not-so-good memory:

Log # 17

Stop #_____ **in State**

_____

Campground: _____

Traveling Companions:

Site #   Reservation #

How Reservation Was Made: Reservation Notes:
         Online   Phone   (Who took it, who made it, how far in
Who recommended this place?   advance?)

Date Arrived: Date Departed:

Day of the Week: Day of the Week:

Time Arrived: Time Departed:

Address: State:

Zip Code: Telephone:

Website: GPS:

Travelled From: Mileage:

Preferred Route: Routes to Avoid:

Sites Along the Way: What Type of Campground?
                                             National Forest   State Park   Private
                                               Army Corps of Engineers   County
                                                  Beurue of Land Mgmt   Other

Rate: Rate Notes: (Discounts, extra fees?)

Deposit Amount:

Types of hookups: Water Hookups?
         Electric ___ Amps ___   Pressure Notes:
      Sewer _____ Dump Station ___

Security Attendant: Yes   No   Gate Code:
When?_____

Showers: Hot Water   Pay Shower
Dry Area   Other _____

Restroom notes:

Pool   Hot Tub   Lodge Room
Game Room

Adult Center   Restaurant
Shuffleboard

Pickleball   Tennis   Mini Golf

Fishing   Gym/Fitness Center

Other Amenities:

Things to Do

What to do while there:

What to do nearby:

Restaurants:

Wildlife we saw:

Nearby campgrounds to consider:

Grocery/General stores nearby:

Pets allowed?

Cell phone service: YES   NO

How many bars of service, usually?

Was the Wi-Fi fast/reliable?

Allow tents?

Scenery:

Weather:

Roads: Paved   Gravel   Dirt

Site Size: Small Medium Large

Parking notes:

Overall Noise Rating: Quiet Light
Road Noise Loud   Train Noises
Loud Road Noise

Ratings: Google ____ Yelp ____ Trip Advisor _____ Campendium _____ Good Sam _____

Our personal rating: ★ ★ ★ ★ ★

A good memory:

A not-so-good memory:

Log # 18

Stop #_____ in State

_____

Campground:

Traveling Companions:

Site #

How Reservation Was Made:
         Online   Phone

Who recommended this place?

Reservation #

Reservation Notes:
(Who took it, who made it, how far in advance?)

Date Arrived:

Day of the Week:

Time Arrived:

Address:

Zip Code:

Website:

Travelled From:

Preferred Route:

Date Departed:

Day of the Week:

Time Departed:

State:

Telephone:

GPS:

Mileage:

Routes to Avoid:

Sites Along the Way:

What Type of Campground?
   National Forest   State Park   Private
      Army Corps of Engineers   County
         Beurue of Land Mgmt   Other

Rate:

Deposit Amount:

Types of hookups:
      Electric ___ Amps ____
   Sewer _____ Dump Station ___

Security Attendant: Yes   No
When?_____

Rate Notes: (Discounts, extra fees?)

Water Hookups?

Pressure Notes:

Gate Code:

Amenities

Showers: Hot Water   Pay Shower
Dry Area   Other _____

Restroom notes:

Pool   Hot Tub   Lodge Room
Game Room

Pickleball   Tennis   Mini Golf

Other Amenities:

Adult Center   Restaurant
Shuffleboard

Fishing   Gym/Fitness Center

Things to Do

What to do while there:

What to do nearby:

Restaurants:

Wildlife we saw:

Nearby campgrounds to consider:

Grocery/General stores nearby:

Pets allowed?

Cell phone service: YES   NO

How many bars of service, usually?

Was the Wi-Fi fast/reliable?

Allow tents?

Scenery:

Weather:

Roads: Paved   Gravel   Dirt

Site Size: Small Medium Large

Parking notes:

Overall Noise Rating: Quiet Light
Road Noise Loud Train Noises
Loud Road Noise

Ratings: Google ـــــ   Yelp ـــــ   Trip Advisor ـــــ   Campendium ـــــ   Good Sam ـــــ

Our personal rating: ★ ★ ★ ★ ★

A good memory:

A not-so-good memory:

Log # 19

Stop #_____ in State

_____

Campground: _____

Traveling Companions:

Site #

How Reservation Was Made:
          Online   Phone

Who recommended this place?

Reservation #

Reservation Notes:
(Who took it, who made it, how far in advance?)

Date Arrived:

Day of the Week:

Time Arrived:

Address:

Zip Code:

Website:

Travelled From:

Preferred Route:

Date Departed:

Day of the Week:

Time Departed:

State:

Telephone:

GPS:

Mileage:

Routes to Avoid:

Sites Along the Way:

What Type of Campground?
   National Forest   State Park   Private
   Army Corps of Engineers   County
      Beurue of Land Mgmt   Other

Rate:

Deposit Amount:

Types of hookups:
        Electric ___ Amps ____
   Sewer _____ Dump Station ___

Security Attendant: Yes   No
When?_____

Rate Notes: (Discounts, extra fees?)

Water Hookups?

Pressure Notes:

Gate Code:

Amenities

Showers: Hot Water   Pay Shower   Restroom notes:
Dry Area   Other _____

    Pool   Hot Tub   Lodge Room   Adult Center   Restaurant
        Game Room   Shuffleboard

    Pickleball   Tennis   Mini Golf   Fishing   Gym/Fitness Center

Other Amenities:

Things to Do

What to do while there: What to do nearby:

Restaurants: Wildlife we saw:

Nearby campgrounds to consider:

Grocery/General stores nearby:

Pets allowed?

Cell phone service: YES   NO   How many bars of service, usually?

Was the Wi-Fi fast/reliable?   Allow tents?

Scenery: Weather:

Roads: Paved   Gravel   Dirt   Site Size: Small Medium Large

Parking notes: Overall Noise Rating: Quiet Light
        Road Noise Loud   Train Noises
        Loud Road Noise

Ratings: Google _____   Yelp _____   Trip Advisor _____   Campendium _____   Good Sam _____

Our personal rating: ★ ★ ★ ★ ★

A good memory:

A not-so-good memory:

Log # 20

Stop #_____ **in State**

_____

Campground:

Traveling Companions:

Site #

How Reservation Was Made:

    Online   Phone

Who recommended this place?

Reservation #

Reservation Notes:

(Who took it, who made it, how far in advance?)

Date Arrived:

Day of the Week:

Time Arrived:

Address:

Zip Code:

Website:

Travelled From:

Preferred Route:

Date Departed:

Day of the Week:

Time Departed:

State:

Telephone:

GPS:

Mileage:

Routes to Avoid:

Sites Along the Way:

What Type of Campground?

    National Forest   State Park   Private

    Army Corps of Engineers   County

        Beurue of Land Mgmt   Other

Rate:

Deposit Amount:

Types of hookups:

        Electric ___ Amps ___

    Sewer _____ Dump Station ___

Security Attendant: Yes   No
When?_____

Rate Notes: (Discounts, extra fees?)

Water Hookups?

Pressure Notes:

Gate Code:

Amenities

Showers: Hot Water   Pay Shower
Dry Area   Other _____

Restroom notes:

Pool   Hot Tub   Lodge Room
Game Room

Adult Center   Restaurant
Shuffleboard

Pickleball   Tennis   Mini Golf

Fishing   Gym/Fitness Center

Other Amenities:

Things to Do

What to do while there:

What to do nearby:

Restaurants:

Wildlife we saw:

Nearby campgrounds to consider:

Grocery/General stores nearby:

Pets allowed?

Cell phone service: YES   NO

How many bars of service, usually?

Was the Wi-Fi fast/reliable?

Allow tents?

Scenery:

Weather:

Roads: Paved   Gravel   Dirt

Site Size: Small Medium Large

Parking notes:

Overall Noise Rating: Quiet Light
Road Noise Loud Train Noises
Loud Road Noise

Ratings: Google _____ Yelp _____ Trip Advisor _____ Campendium _____ Good Sam _____

Our personal rating: ★ ★ ★ ★ ★

A good memory:

A not-so-good memory:

Log # 21

Stop #_____ in State

_____

Campground:

Traveling Companions:

Site #

How Reservation Was Made:

      Online   Phone

Who recommended this place?

Reservation #

Reservation Notes:

(Who took it, who made it, how far in advance?)

Date Arrived:

Day of the Week:

Time Arrived:

Address:

Zip Code:

Website:

Travelled From:

Preferred Route:

Date Departed:

Day of the Week:

Time Departed:

State:

Telephone:

GPS:

Mileage:

Routes to Avoid:

Sites Along the Way:

What Type of Campground?

   National Forest State Park Private

    Army Corps of Engineers County

      Beurue of Land Mgmt Other

Rate:

Deposit Amount:

Types of hookups:

     Electric ___ Amps ____

   Sewer _____ Dump Station ___

Security Attendant: Yes No

When?_____

Rate Notes: (Discounts, extra fees?)

Water Hookups?

Pressure Notes:

Gate Code:

Amenities

Showers: Hot Water   Pay Shower
Dry Area   Other _____

Pool   Hot Tub   Lodge Room
Game Room

Pickleball   Tennis   Mini Golf

Other Amenities:

Restroom notes:

Adult Center   Restaurant
Shuffleboard

Fishing   Gym/Fitness Center

Things to Do

What to do while there:

What to do nearby:

Restaurants:

Wildlife we saw:

Nearby campgrounds to consider:

Grocery/General stores nearby:

Pets allowed?

Cell phone service: YES   NO

How many bars of service, usually?

Was the Wi-Fi fast/reliable?

Allow tents?

Scenery:

Weather:

Roads: Paved   Gravel   Dirt

Site Size: Small Medium Large

Parking notes:

Overall Noise Rating: Quiet Light
Road Noise Loud   Train Noises
Loud Road Noise

Ratings: Google _____ Yelp _____ Trip Advisor _____ Campendium _____ Good Sam _____

Our personal rating: ★ ★ ★ ★ ★

A good memory:

A not-so-good memory:

Log # 22

Stop #_____
in
State

_____

Campground:

Traveling Companions:

Site #   Reservation #

How Reservation Was Made: Reservation Notes:
            Online   Phone   (Who took it, who made it, how far in
Who recommended this place?   advance?)

Date Arrived: Date Departed:

Day of the Week: Day of the Week:

Time Arrived: Time Departed:

Address: State:

Zip Code: Telephone:

Website: GPS:

Travelled From: Mileage:

Preferred Route: Routes to Avoid:

Sites Along the Way: What Type of Campground?
                                              National Forest   State Park   Private
                                              Army Corps of Engineers   County
                                                   Beurue of Land Mgmt   Other

Rate: Rate Notes: (Discounts, extra fees?)

Deposit Amount:

Types of hookups: Water Hookups?
            Electric ___ Amps ___   Pressure Notes:
        Sewer _____ Dump Station ___

Security Attendant: Yes   No   Gate Code:
When?_____

Amenities

Showers: Hot Water   Pay Shower
Dry Area   Other _____

Restroom notes:

        Pool   Hot Tub   Lodge Room
                Game Room

        Adult Center   Restaurant
                Shuffleboard

        Pickleball   Tennis   Mini Golf

Fishing   Gym/Fitness Center

Other Amenities:

Things to Do

What to do while there:

What to do nearby:

Restaurants:

Wildlife we saw:

Nearby campgrounds to consider:

Grocery/General stores nearby:

Pets allowed?

Cell phone service: YES   NO

How many bars of service, usually?

Was the Wi-Fi fast/reliable?

Allow tents?

Scenery:

Weather:

Roads: Paved   Gravel   Dirt

Site Size: Small Medium Large

Parking notes:

Overall Noise Rating: Quiet Light
Road Noise Loud   Train Noises
        Loud Road Noise

Ratings: Google _____ Yelp _____ Trip Advisor _____ Campendium _____ Good Sam _____

Our personal rating: ★ ★ ★ ★ ★

A good memory:

A not-so-good memory:

Log # 23

Stop #_____ in State

_____

Traveling Companions:

Site #

How Reservation Was Made:
          Online   Phone

Who recommended this place?

Reservation #

Reservation Notes:
(Who took it, who made it, how far in advance?)

Date Arrived:

Day of the Week:

Time Arrived:

Address:

Zip Code:

Website:

Travelled From:

Preferred Route:

Date Departed:

Day of the Week:

Time Departed:

State:

Telephone:

GPS:

Mileage:

Routes to Avoid:

Sites Along the Way:

What Type of Campground?
   National Forest   State Park   Private
   Army Corps of Engineers   County
      Beurue of Land Mgmt   Other

Rate:

Deposit Amount:

Types of hookups:
        Electric ___ Amps ___
   Sewer _____ Dump Station ___

Security Attendant: Yes   No
When?_____

Rate Notes: (Discounts, extra fees?)

Water Hookups?

Pressure Notes:

Gate Code:

Showers: Hot Water   Pay Shower
Dry Area   Other _____

    Pool   Hot Tub   Lodge Room
          Game Room

    Pickleball   Tennis   Mini Golf

Other Amenities:

Restroom notes:

    Adult Center   Restaurant
          Shuffleboard

Fishing   Gym/Fitness Center

Things to Do

What to do while there:

What to do nearby:

Restaurants:

Wildlife we saw:

Nearby campgrounds to consider:

Grocery/General stores nearby:

Pets allowed?

Cell phone service: YES   NO

How many bars of service, usually?

Was the Wi-Fi fast/reliable?

Allow tents?

Scenery:

Weather:

Roads: Paved   Gravel   Dirt

Site Size: Small Medium Large

Parking notes:

Overall Noise Rating: Quiet Light
Road Noise Loud Train Noises
Loud Road Noise

Ratings: Google _____ Yelp _____ Trip Advisor _____ Campendium _____ Good Sam _____

Our personal rating: ★ ★ ★ ★ ★

A good memory:

A not-so-good memory:

Log # 24

Stop #_____
in
State

_____

Campground:

Traveling Companions:

Site #

How Reservation Was Made:
        Online   Phone
Who recommended this place?

Reservation #

Reservation Notes:
(Who took it, who made it, how far in advance?)

Date Arrived:

Day of the Week:

Time Arrived:

Address:

Zip Code:

Website:

Travelled From:

Preferred Route:

Date Departed:

Day of the Week:

Time Departed:

State:

Telephone:

GPS:

Mileage:

Routes to Avoid:

Sites Along the Way:

What Type of Campground?
    National Forest   State Park   Private
        Army Corps of Engineers   County
            Beurue of Land Mgmt   Other

Rate:

Deposit Amount:

Types of hookups:
        Electric ___ Amps ____
    Sewer _____ Dump Station ___

Security Attendant: Yes   No
When?_____

Rate Notes: (Discounts, extra fees?)

Water Hookups?

Pressure Notes:

Gate Code:

Amenities

Showers: Hot Water   Pay Shower
Dry Area   Other _____

    Pool   Hot Tub   Lodge Room
            Game Room

    Pickleball   Tennis   Mini Golf

Other Amenities:

Restroom notes:

    Adult Center   Restaurant
         Shuffleboard

  Fishing   Gym/Fitness Center

Things to Do

What to do while there:

What to do nearby:

Restaurants:

Wildlife we saw:

Nearby campgrounds to consider:

Grocery/General stores nearby:

Pets allowed?

Cell phone service: YES   NO

How many bars of service, usually?

Was the Wi-Fi fast/reliable?

Allow tents?

Scenery:

Weather:

Roads: Paved   Gravel   Dirt

Site Size: Small Medium Large

Parking notes:

Overall Noise Rating: Quiet Light
Road Noise Loud   Train Noises
Loud Road Noise

Ratings: Google _____ Yelp _____ Trip Advisor _____ Campendium _____ Good Sam _____

Our personal rating: ⭐ ⭐ ⭐ ⭐ ⭐

A good memory:

A not-so-good memory:

Log # 25

Stop #_____
in
State
_____

Campground: _____

Traveling Companions:

Site #

Reservation #

How Reservation Was Made:
        Online   Phone

Reservation Notes:
(Who took it, who made it, how far in advance?)

Who recommended this place?

Date Arrived:

Date Departed:

Day of the Week:

Day of the Week:

Time Arrived:

Time Departed:

Address:

State:

Zip Code:

Telephone:

Website:

GPS:

Travelled From:

Mileage:

Preferred Route:

Routes to Avoid:

Sites Along the Way:

What Type of Campground?
    National Forest   State Park   Private
    Army Corps of Engineers   County
        Beurue of Land Mgmt   Other

Rate:

Rate Notes: (Discounts, extra fees?)

Deposit Amount:

Types of hookups:
        Electric ___ Amps ____
    Sewer _____ Dump Station ___

Water Hookups?

Pressure Notes:

Security Attendant: Yes   No
When?_____

Gate Code:

Amenities

Showers: Hot Water   Pay Shower
Dry Area   Other _____

    Pool   Hot Tub   Lodge Room
          Game Room

    Pickleball   Tennis   Mini Golf

Other Amenities:

Restroom notes:

    Adult Center   Restaurant
        Shuffleboard

    Fishing   Gym/Fitness Center

Things to Do

What to do while there:

What to do nearby:

Restaurants:

Wildlife we saw:

Nearby campgrounds to consider:

Grocery/General stores nearby:

Pets allowed?

Cell phone service: YES   NO

How many bars of service, usually?

Was the Wi-Fi fast/reliable?

Allow tents?

Scenery:

Weather:

Roads: Paved   Gravel   Dirt

Site Size: Small Medium Large

Parking notes:

Overall Noise Rating: Quiet Light
Road Noise Loud   Train Noises
Loud Road Noise

Ratings: Google _____ Yelp _____ Trip Advisor _____ Campendium _____ Good Sam _____

Our personal rating: ★ ★ ★ ★ ★

A good memory:

A not-so-good memory:

Log # 26

Stop #_____ **in State**

_____

Campground:

Traveling Companions:

Site #

Reservation #

How Reservation Was Made:
        Online   Phone

Reservation Notes:
(Who took it, who made it, how far in advance?)

Who recommended this place?

Date Arrived:

Date Departed:

Day of the Week:

Day of the Week:

Time Arrived:

Time Departed:

Address:

State:

Zip Code:

Telephone:

Website:

GPS:

Travelled From:

Mileage:

Preferred Route:

Routes to Avoid:

Sites Along the Way:

What Type of Campground?
   National Forest State Park Private
    Army Corps of Engineers County
     Beurue of Land Mgmt Other

Rate:

Rate Notes: (Discounts, extra fees?)

Deposit Amount:

Types of hookups:
     Electric ____ Amps ____
   Sewer _____ Dump Station ___

Water Hookups?

Pressure Notes:

Security Attendant: Yes No
When?_____

Gate Code:

Amenities

Showers: Hot Water   Pay Shower   Dry Area   Other _____

Restroom notes:

Pool   Hot Tub   Lodge Room   Game Room

Adult Center   Restaurant   Shuffleboard

Pickleball   Tennis   Mini Golf

Fishing   Gym/Fitness Center

Other Amenities:

Things to Do

What to do while there:

What to do nearby:

Restaurants:

Wildlife we saw:

Nearby campgrounds to consider:

Grocery/General stores nearby:

Pets allowed?

Cell phone service: YES   NO

How many bars of service, usually?

Was the Wi-Fi fast/reliable?

Allow tents?

Scenery:

Weather:

Roads: Paved   Gravel   Dirt

Site Size: Small Medium Large

Parking notes:

Overall Noise Rating: Quiet Light   Road Noise Loud   Train Noises   Loud Road Noise

Ratings: Google _____ Yelp _____ Trip Advisor _____ Campendium _____ Good Sam _____

Our personal rating: ★ ★ ★ ★ ★

A good memory:

A not-so-good memory:

Log # 27

Stop #_____ **in State**

_____

Traveling Companions:

Site #   Reservation #

How Reservation Was Made: Reservation Notes:
      Online   Phone   (Who took it, who made it, how far in
Who recommended this place?   advance?)

Date Arrived: Date Departed:

Day of the Week: Day of the Week:

Time Arrived: Time Departed:

Address: State:

Zip Code: Telephone:

Website: GPS:

Travelled From: Mileage:

Preferred Route: Routes to Avoid:

Sites Along the Way: What Type of Campground?
        National Forest   State Park   Private
        Army Corps of Engineers   County
        Beurue of Land Mgmt   Other

Rate: Rate Notes: (Discounts, extra fees?)

Deposit Amount:

Types of hookups: Water Hookups?
     Electric ___ Amps ____   Pressure Notes:
  Sewer _____ Dump Station ___

Security Attendant: Yes   No   Gate Code:
When?_____

Amenities

Showers: Hot Water   Pay Shower
Dry Area   Other _____

Restroom notes:

     Pool   Hot Tub   Lodge Room
          Game Room

     Adult Center   Restaurant
         Shuffleboard

     Pickleball   Tennis   Mini Golf

Fishing   Gym/Fitness Center

Other Amenities:

Things to Do

What to do while there:

What to do nearby:

Restaurants:

Wildlife we saw:

Nearby campgrounds to consider:

Grocery/General stores nearby:

Pets allowed?

Cell phone service: YES   NO

How many bars of service, usually?

Was the Wi-Fi fast/reliable?

Allow tents?

Scenery:

Weather:

Roads: Paved   Gravel   Dirt

Site Size: Small Medium Large

Parking notes:

Overall Noise Rating: Quiet Light
Road Noise Loud Train Noises
Loud Road Noise

Ratings: Google ____ Yelp ____ Trip Advisor ____ Campendium ____ Good Sam ____

Our personal rating: ★ ★ ★ ★ ★

A good memory:

A not-so-good memory:

Log # 28

Stop #_____
in
State

_____

Campground:

Traveling Companions:

Site #

How Reservation Was Made:

Online   Phone

Who recommended this place?

Reservation #

Reservation Notes:

(Who took it, who made it, how far in advance?)

Date Arrived:

Day of the Week:

Time Arrived:

Address:

Zip Code:

Website:

Travelled From:

Preferred Route:

Date Departed:

Day of the Week:

Time Departed:

State:

Telephone:

GPS:

Mileage:

Routes to Avoid:

Sites Along the Way:

What Type of Campground?

National Forest   State Park   Private
Army Corps of Engineers   County
Beurue of Land Mgmt   Other

Rate:

Deposit Amount:

Types of hookups:

Electric ___ Amps ___

Sewer _____ Dump Station ___

Security Attendant: Yes   No
When?_____

Rate Notes: (Discounts, extra fees?)

Water Hookups?

Pressure Notes:

Gate Code:

Amenities

Showers: Hot Water   Pay Shower
Dry Area   Other _____

Pool   Hot Tub   Lodge Room
Game Room

Pickleball   Tennis   Mini Golf

Other Amenities:

Restroom notes:

Adult Center   Restaurant
Shuffleboard

Fishing   Gym/Fitness Center

Things to Do

What to do while there:

What to do nearby:

Restaurants:

Wildlife we saw:

Nearby campgrounds to consider:

Grocery/General stores nearby:

Pets allowed?

Cell phone service: YES   NO

How many bars of service, usually?

Was the Wi-Fi fast/reliable?

Allow tents?

Scenery:

Weather:

Roads: Paved   Gravel   Dirt

Site Size: Small Medium Large

Parking notes:

Overall Noise Rating: Quiet Light
Road Noise Loud   Train Noises
Loud Road Noise

Ratings: Google ____ Yelp ____ Trip Advisor _____ Campendium _____ Good Sam _____

Our personal rating: ⭐ ⭐ ⭐ ⭐ ⭐

A good memory:

A not-so-good memory:

Log # 29

Stop #_____ **in State**
_____

Campground:
_____

Traveling Companions:

Site #   Reservation #

How Reservation Was Made: Reservation Notes:
          Online   Phone   (Who took it, who made it, how far in
Who recommended this place?   advance?)

Date Arrived: Date Departed:

Day of the Week: Day of the Week:

Time Arrived: Time Departed:

Address: State:

Zip Code: Telephone:

Website: GPS:

Travelled From: Mileage:

Preferred Route: Routes to Avoid:

Sites Along the Way: What Type of Campground?
                                                National Forest   State Park   Private
                                                Army Corps of Engineers   County
                                                   Beurue of Land Mgmt   Other

Rate: Rate Notes: (Discounts, extra fees?)

Deposit Amount:

Types of hookups: Water Hookups?
          Electric ___ Amps _____   Pressure Notes:
     Sewer _____ Dump Station ___

Security Attendant: Yes   No   Gate Code:
When?_____

Amenities

Showers: Hot Water   Pay Shower   Dry Area   Other _____

Restroom notes:

Pool   Hot Tub   Lodge Room   Game Room

Adult Center   Restaurant   Shuffleboard

Pickleball   Tennis   Mini Golf

Fishing   Gym/Fitness Center

Other Amenities:

Things to Do

What to do while there:

What to do nearby:

Restaurants:

Wildlife we saw:

Nearby campgrounds to consider:

Grocery/General stores nearby:

Pets allowed?

Cell phone service: YES   NO

How many bars of service, usually?

Was the Wi-Fi fast/reliable?

Allow tents?

Scenery:

Weather:

Roads: Paved   Gravel   Dirt

Site Size: Small Medium Large

Parking notes:

Overall Noise Rating: Quiet Light Road Noise Loud   Train Noises Loud Road Noise

Ratings: Google _____   Yelp _____ Trip Advisor _____   Campendium _____   Good Sam _____

Our personal rating: ★ ★ ★ ★ ★

A good memory:

A not-so-good memory:

Log # 30

Stop #_____ in State

_____

Campground:

Traveling Companions:

Site #

How Reservation Was Made:
          Online   Phone

Who recommended this place?

Reservation #

Reservation Notes:
(Who took it, who made it, how far in advance?)

Date Arrived:

Day of the Week:

Time Arrived:

Address:

Zip Code:

Website:

Travelled From:

Preferred Route:

Date Departed:

Day of the Week:

Time Departed:

State:

Telephone:

GPS:

Mileage:

Routes to Avoid:

Sites Along the Way:

What Type of Campground?
   National Forest   State Park   Private
      Army Corps of Engineers   County
         Beurue of Land Mgmt   Other

Rate:

Deposit Amount:

Types of hookups:
          Electric ___ Amps ____
      Sewer _____ Dump Station ___

Security Attendant: Yes   No
When?_____

Rate Notes: (Discounts, extra fees?)

Water Hookups?

Pressure Notes:

Gate Code:

Amenities

Showers: Hot Water   Pay Shower
Dry Area   Other _____

    Pool   Hot Tub   Lodge Room
          Game Room

    Pickleball   Tennis   Mini Golf

Other Amenities:

Restroom notes:

    Adult Center   Restaurant
         Shuffleboard

Fishing   Gym/Fitness Center

Things to Do

What to do while there:

What to do nearby:

Restaurants:

Wildlife we saw:

Nearby campgrounds to consider:

Grocery/General stores nearby:

Pets allowed?

Cell phone service: YES   NO

How many bars of service, usually?

Was the Wi-Fi fast/reliable?

Allow tents?

Scenery:

Weather:

Roads: Paved   Gravel   Dirt

Site Size: Small Medium Large

Parking notes:

Overall Noise Rating: Quiet Light
Road Noise Loud   Train Noises
Loud Road Noise

Ratings: Google _____ Yelp _____ Trip Advisor _____ Campendium _____ Good Sam _____

Our personal rating: ★ ★ ★ ★ ★

A good memory:

A not-so-good memory:

Log # 31

Stop # _____ in State

_____

Campground:

Traveling Companions:

Site #

How Reservation Was Made:

Online   Phone

Who recommended this place?

Reservation #

Reservation Notes:

(Who took it, who made it, how far in advance?)

Date Arrived:

Day of the Week:

Time Arrived:

Address:

Zip Code:

Website:

Travelled From:

Preferred Route:

Date Departed:

Day of the Week:

Time Departed:

State:

Telephone:

GPS:

Mileage:

Routes to Avoid:

Sites Along the Way:

What Type of Campground?

National Forest   State Park   Private
Army Corps of Engineers   County
Beurue of Land Mgmt   Other

Rate:

Deposit Amount:

Types of hookups:

Electric ___ Amps ____

Sewer _____ Dump Station ___

Security Attendant: Yes   No
When?_____

Rate Notes: (Discounts, extra fees?)

Water Hookups?

Pressure Notes:

Gate Code:

Amenities

Showers: Hot Water   Pay Shower
Dry Area   Other _____

Pool   Hot Tub   Lodge Room
Game Room

Pickleball   Tennis   Mini Golf

Other Amenities:

Restroom notes:

Adult Center   Restaurant
Shuffleboard

Fishing   Gym/Fitness Center

Things to Do

What to do while there:

What to do nearby:

Restaurants:

Wildlife we saw:

Nearby campgrounds to consider:

Grocery/General stores nearby:

Pets allowed?

Cell phone service: YES   NO

How many bars of service, usually?

Was the Wi-Fi fast/reliable?

Allow tents?

Scenery:

Weather:

Roads: Paved   Gravel   Dirt

Site Size: Small Medium Large

Parking notes:

Overall Noise Rating: Quiet Light
Road Noise Loud Train Noises
Loud Road Noise

Ratings: Google _____ Yelp _____ Trip Advisor _____ Campendium _____ Good Sam _____

Our personal rating: ⭐ ⭐ ⭐ ⭐ ⭐

A good memory:

A not-so-good memory:

Log # 32

Stop #_____ in State

_____

Campground:
_____

Traveling Companions:

Site #   Reservation #

How Reservation Was Made: Reservation Notes:
          Online   Phone   (Who took it, who made it, how far in
Who recommended this place?   advance?)

Date Arrived: Date Departed:

Day of the Week: Day of the Week:

Time Arrived: Time Departed:

Address: State:

Zip Code: Telephone:

Website: GPS:

Travelled From: Mileage:

Preferred Route: Routes to Avoid:

Sites Along the Way: What Type of Campground?
                                            National Forest State Park Private
                                            Army Corps of Engineers County
                                              Beurue of Land Mgmt Other

Rate: Rate Notes: (Discounts, extra fees?)

Deposit Amount:

Types of hookups: Water Hookups?
        Electric ___ Amps ___   Pressure Notes:
    Sewer _____ Dump Station ___

Security Attendant: Yes No   Gate Code:
When?_____

Showers: Hot Water   Pay Shower
Dry Area   Other _____

Restroom notes:

Pool   Hot Tub   Lodge Room
Game Room

Adult Center   Restaurant
Shuffleboard

Pickleball   Tennis   Mini Golf

Fishing   Gym/Fitness Center

Other Amenities:

Things to Do

What to do while there:

What to do nearby:

Restaurants:

Wildlife we saw:

Nearby campgrounds to consider:

Grocery/General stores nearby:

Pets allowed?

Cell phone service: YES   NO

How many bars of service, usually?

Was the Wi-Fi fast/reliable?

Allow tents?

Scenery:

Weather:

Roads: Paved   Gravel   Dirt

Site Size: Small Medium Large

Parking notes:

Overall Noise Rating: Quiet Light
Road Noise Loud Train Noises
Loud Road Noise

Ratings: Google ____ Yelp ____ Trip Advisor ____ Campendium ____ Good Sam ____

Our personal rating: ★ ★ ★ ★ ★

A good memory:

A not-so-good memory:

Log # 33

Stop #_____
in State
_____

Campground:

Traveling Companions:

Site #

How Reservation Was Made:
          Online   Phone

Who recommended this place?

Reservation #

Reservation Notes:
(Who took it, who made it, how far in advance?)

Date Arrived:

Day of the Week:

Time Arrived:

Address:

Zip Code:

Website:

Travelled From:

Preferred Route:

Date Departed:

Day of the Week:

Time Departed:

State:

Telephone:

GPS:

Mileage:

Routes to Avoid:

Sites Along the Way:

What Type of Campground?
    National Forest   State Park   Private
      Army Corps of Engineers   County
          Beurue of Land Mgmt   Other

Rate:

Deposit Amount:

Types of hookups:
        Electric ___ Amps _____
    Sewer _____ Dump Station ___

Security Attendant: Yes   No
When?_____

Rate Notes: (Discounts, extra fees?)

Water Hookups?

Pressure Notes:

Gate Code:

Amenities

Showers: Hot Water   Pay Shower
Dry Area   Other _____

Restroom notes:

Pool   Hot Tub   Lodge Room
Game Room

Adult Center   Restaurant
Shuffleboard

Pickleball   Tennis   Mini Golf

Fishing   Gym/Fitness Center

Other Amenities:

Things to Do

What to do while there:

What to do nearby:

Restaurants:

Wildlife we saw:

Nearby campgrounds to consider:

Grocery/General stores nearby:

Pets allowed?

Cell phone service: YES   NO

How many bars of service, usually?

Was the Wi-Fi fast/reliable?

Allow tents?

Scenery:

Weather:

Roads: Paved   Gravel   Dirt

Site Size: Small Medium Large

Parking notes:

Overall Noise Rating: Quiet Light
Road Noise Loud Train Noises
Loud Road Noise

Ratings: Google _____ Yelp _____ Trip Advisor _____ Campendium _____ Good Sam _____

Our personal rating: ⭐ ⭐ ⭐ ⭐ ⭐

A good memory:

A not-so-good memory:

Log # 34

Stop #_____ in State

_____

Campground:

Traveling Companions:

Site #

How Reservation Was Made:
          Online   Phone
Who recommended this place?

Reservation #

Reservation Notes:
(Who took it, who made it, how far in advance?)

Date Arrived:

Day of the Week:

Time Arrived:

Address:

Zip Code:

Website:

Travelled From:

Preferred Route:

Date Departed:

Day of the Week:

Time Departed:

State:

Telephone:

GPS:

Mileage:

Routes to Avoid:

Sites Along the Way:

What Type of Campground?
    National Forest   State Park   Private
    Army Corps of Engineers   County
        Beurue of Land Mgmt   Other

Rate:

Deposit Amount:

Types of hookups:
        Electric ___ Amps ____
    Sewer _____ Dump Station ___

Security Attendant: Yes   No
When?_____

Rate Notes: (Discounts, extra fees?)

Water Hookups?

Pressure Notes:

Gate Code:

Amenities

Showers: Hot Water   Pay Shower
Dry Area   Other _____

    Pool   Hot Tub   Lodge Room
        Game Room

    Pickleball   Tennis   Mini Golf

Other Amenities:

Restroom notes:

    Adult Center   Restaurant
        Shuffleboard

Fishing   Gym/Fitness Center

Things to Do

What to do while there:

What to do nearby:

Restaurants:

Wildlife we saw:

Nearby campgrounds to consider:

Grocery/General stores nearby:

Pets allowed?

Cell phone service: YES   NO

How many bars of service, usually?

Was the Wi-Fi fast/reliable?

Allow tents?

Scenery:

Weather:

Roads: Paved   Gravel   Dirt

Site Size: Small Medium Large

Parking notes:

Overall Noise Rating: Quiet Light
Road Noise Loud   Train Noises
Loud Road Noise

Ratings: Google _____ Yelp _____ Trip Advisor _____ Campendium _____ Good Sam _____

Our personal rating: ★ ★ ★ ★ ★

A good memory:

A not-so-good memory:

Log # 35

Stop #_____ **in State**

_____

Campground: _____

Traveling Companions:

Site #

How Reservation Was Made:
        Online   Phone

Who recommended this place?

Reservation #

Reservation Notes:
(Who took it, who made it, how far in advance?)

Date Arrived:

Day of the Week:

Time Arrived:

Address:

Zip Code:

Website:

Travelled From:

Preferred Route:

Date Departed:

Day of the Week:

Time Departed:

State:

Telephone:

GPS:

Mileage:

Routes to Avoid:

Sites Along the Way:

What Type of Campground?
    National Forest   State Park   Private
    Army Corps of Engineers   County
        Beurue of Land Mgmt   Other

Rate:

Deposit Amount:

Types of hookups:
        Electric ___ Amps _____
    Sewer _____ Dump Station ___

Security Attendant: Yes   No
When?_____

Rate Notes: (Discounts, extra fees?)

Water Hookups?

Pressure Notes:

Gate Code:

Showers: Hot Water   Pay Shower
Dry Area   Other _____

Restroom notes:

Pool   Hot Tub   Lodge Room
Game Room

Adult Center   Restaurant
Shuffleboard

Pickleball   Tennis   Mini Golf

Fishing   Gym/Fitness Center

Other Amenities:

Things to Do

What to do while there:

What to do nearby:

Restaurants:

Wildlife we saw:

Nearby campgrounds to consider:

Grocery/General stores nearby:

Pets allowed?

Cell phone service: YES   NO

How many bars of service, usually?

Was the Wi-Fi fast/reliable?

Allow tents?

Scenery:

Weather:

Roads: Paved   Gravel   Dirt

Site Size: Small Medium Large

Parking notes:

Overall Noise Rating: Quiet Light
Road Noise Loud Train Noises
Loud Road Noise

Ratings: Google _____ Yelp _____ Trip Advisor _____ Campendium _____ Good Sam _____

Our personal rating: ⭐ ⭐ ⭐ ⭐ ⭐

A good memory:

A not-so-good memory:

Log # 36

Stop #_____
in
State

_____

Campground: _____

Traveling Companions:

Site #   Reservation #

How Reservation Was Made: Reservation Notes:
        Online   Phone   (Who took it, who made it, how far in
Who recommended this place?   advance?)

Date Arrived: Date Departed:

Day of the Week: Day of the Week:

Time Arrived: Time Departed:

Address: State:

Zip Code: Telephone:

Website: GPS:

Travelled From: Mileage:

Preferred Route: Routes to Avoid:

Sites Along the Way: What Type of Campground?
    National Forest State Park Private
    Army Corps of Engineers County
    Beurue of Land Mgmt Other

Rate: Rate Notes: (Discounts, extra fees?)

Deposit Amount:

Types of hookups: Water Hookups?
    Electric ____ Amps ____   Pressure Notes:
  Sewer _____ Dump Station ___

Security Attendant: Yes   No   Gate Code:
When?_____

Amenities

Showers: Hot Water   Pay Shower
Dry Area   Other _____

    Pool   Hot Tub   Lodge Room
        Game Room

    Pickleball   Tennis   Mini Golf

Other Amenities:

Restroom notes:

    Adult Center   Restaurant
        Shuffleboard

  Fishing   Gym/Fitness Center

Things to Do

What to do while there:

What to do nearby:

Restaurants:

Wildlife we saw:

Nearby campgrounds to consider:

Grocery/General stores nearby:

Pets allowed?

Cell phone service: YES   NO

How many bars of service, usually?

Was the Wi-Fi fast/reliable?

Allow tents?

Scenery:

Weather:

Roads: Paved   Gravel   Dirt

Site Size: Small Medium Large

Parking notes:

Overall Noise Rating: Quiet Light
Road Noise Loud Train Noises
Loud Road Noise

Ratings: Google ____ Yelp ____ Trip Advisor ____ Campendium ____ Good Sam ____

Our personal rating: ⭐ ⭐ ⭐ ⭐ ⭐

A good memory:

A not-so-good memory:

Log # 37

Stop #_____ in State

_____

Campground:

Traveling Companions:

Site #

How Reservation Was Made:
          Online   Phone
Who recommended this place?

Reservation #

Reservation Notes:
(Who took it, who made it, how far in advance?)

Date Arrived:

Day of the Week:

Time Arrived:

Address:

Zip Code:

Website:

Travelled From:

Preferred Route:

Date Departed:

Day of the Week:

Time Departed:

State:

Telephone:

GPS:

Mileage:

Routes to Avoid:

Sites Along the Way:

What Type of Campground?
   National Forest   State Park   Private
   Army Corps of Engineers   County
      Beurue of Land Mgmt   Other

Rate:

Deposit Amount:

Types of hookups:
        Electric ___ Amps ____
    Sewer _____ Dump Station ____

Rate Notes: (Discounts, extra fees?)

Water Hookups?

Pressure Notes:

Security Attendant: Yes   No
When?_____

Gate Code:

Amenities

Showers: Hot Water   Pay Shower
Dry Area   Other _____

Restroom notes:

Pool   Hot Tub   Lodge Room
Game Room

Adult Center   Restaurant
Shuffleboard

Pickleball   Tennis   Mini Golf

Fishing   Gym/Fitness Center

Other Amenities:

Things to Do

What to do while there:

What to do nearby:

Restaurants:

Wildlife we saw:

Nearby campgrounds to consider:

Grocery/General stores nearby:

Pets allowed?

Cell phone service: YES   NO

How many bars of service, usually?

Was the Wi-Fi fast/reliable?

Allow tents?

Scenery:

Weather:

Roads: Paved   Gravel   Dirt

Site Size: Small Medium Large

Parking notes:

Overall Noise Rating: Quiet Light
Road Noise Loud Train Noises
Loud Road Noise

Ratings: Google _____ Yelp _____ Trip Advisor _____ Campendium _____ Good Sam _____

Our personal rating: ★ ★ ★ ★ ★

A good memory:

A not-so-good memory:

Log # 38

Stop #_____ **in State**

_____

Campground:

Traveling Companions:

Site #

How Reservation Was Made:

      Online   Phone

Who recommended this place?

Reservation #

Reservation Notes:

(Who took it, who made it, how far in advance?)

Date Arrived:

Day of the Week:

Time Arrived:

Address:

Zip Code:

Website:

Travelled From:

Preferred Route:

Date Departed:

Day of the Week:

Time Departed:

State:

Telephone:

GPS:

Mileage:

Routes to Avoid:

Sites Along the Way:

What Type of Campground?

   National Forest State Park Private

   Army Corps of Engineers County

    Beurue of Land Mgmt Other

Rate:

Deposit Amount:

Types of hookups:

    Electric ___ Amps ____

  Sewer _____ Dump Station ___

Security Attendant: Yes No

When?_____

Rate Notes: (Discounts, extra fees?)

Water Hookups?

Pressure Notes:

Gate Code:

Amenities

Showers: Hot Water   Pay Shower
Dry Area   Other _____

    Pool   Hot Tub   Lodge Room
           Game Room

    Pickleball   Tennis   Mini Golf

Other Amenities:

Restroom notes:

    Adult Center   Restaurant
         Shuffleboard

    Fishing   Gym/Fitness Center

Things to Do

What to do while there:

What to do nearby:

Restaurants:

Wildlife we saw:

Nearby campgrounds to consider:

Grocery/General stores nearby:

Pets allowed?

Cell phone service: YES   NO

How many bars of service, usually?

Was the Wi-Fi fast/reliable?

Allow tents?

Scenery:

Weather:

Roads: Paved   Gravel   Dirt

Site Size: Small Medium Large

Parking notes:

Overall Noise Rating: Quiet Light
Road Noise Loud   Train Noises
Loud Road Noise

Ratings: Google _____ Yelp _____ Trip Advisor _____ Campendium _____ Good Sam _____

Our personal rating: ★ ★ ★ ★ ★

A good memory:

A not-so-good memory:

Log # 39

Stop #_____
in
State
_____

Campground: _____

Traveling Companions:

Site #   Reservation #

How Reservation Was Made: Reservation Notes:
        Online   Phone   (Who took it, who made it, how far in advance?)
Who recommended this place?

Date Arrived: Date Departed:

Day of the Week: Day of the Week:

Time Arrived: Time Departed:

Address: State:

Zip Code: Telephone:

Website: GPS:

Travelled From: Mileage:

Preferred Route: Routes to Avoid:

Sites Along the Way: What Type of Campground?
                                    National Forest   State Park   Private
                                    Army Corps of Engineers   County
                                        Beurue of Land Mgmt   Other

Rate: Rate Notes: (Discounts, extra fees?)

Deposit Amount:

Types of hookups: Water Hookups?
        Electric ___ Amps ___   Pressure Notes:
    Sewer _____ Dump Station ___

Security Attendant: Yes   No   Gate Code:
When?_____

Amenities

Showers: Hot Water   Pay Shower
Dry Area   Other _____

Restroom notes:

Pool   Hot Tub   Lodge Room
Game Room

Adult Center   Restaurant
Shuffleboard

Pickleball   Tennis   Mini Golf

Fishing   Gym/Fitness Center

Other Amenities:

Things to Do

What to do while there:

What to do nearby:

Restaurants:

Wildlife we saw:

Nearby campgrounds to consider:

Grocery/General stores nearby:

Pets allowed?

Cell phone service: YES   NO

How many bars of service, usually?

Was the Wi-Fi fast/reliable?

Allow tents?

Scenery:

Weather:

Roads: Paved   Gravel   Dirt

Site Size: Small Medium Large

Parking notes:

Overall Noise Rating: Quiet Light
Road Noise Loud   Train Noises
Loud Road Noise

Ratings: Google _____   Yelp _____ Trip Advisor _____   Campendium _____   Good Sam _____

Our personal rating: ★ ★ ★ ★ ★

A good memory:

A not-so-good memory:

Log # 40

Stop #_____
in
State

_____

Campground: _____

Traveling Companions:

Site # _____   Reservation # _____

How Reservation Was Made: Reservation Notes:
        Online   Phone   (Who took it, who made it, how far in advance?)
Who recommended this place?

Date Arrived: Date Departed:
Day of the Week: Day of the Week:
Time Arrived: Time Departed:
Address: State:
Zip Code: Telephone:
Website: GPS:
Travelled From: Mileage:
Preferred Route: Routes to Avoid:

Sites Along the Way: What Type of Campground?
                                     National Forest   State Park   Private
                                     Army Corps of Engineers   County
                                         Beurue of Land Mgmt   Other

Rate: Rate Notes: (Discounts, extra fees?)
Deposit Amount:
Types of hookups: Water Hookups?
        Electric ___ Amps ____   Pressure Notes:
    Sewer _____ Dump Station ___
Security Attendant: Yes   No   Gate Code:
When?_____

Amenities

Showers: Hot Water   Pay Shower
Dry Area   Other _____

    Pool   Hot Tub   Lodge Room
        Game Room

    Pickleball   Tennis   Mini Golf

Other Amenities:

Restroom notes:

    Adult Center   Restaurant
        Shuffleboard

    Fishing   Gym/Fitness Center

Things to Do

What to do while there:

What to do nearby:

Restaurants:

Wildlife we saw:

Nearby campgrounds to consider:

Grocery/General stores nearby:

Pets allowed?

Cell phone service: YES   NO

How many bars of service, usually?

Was the Wi-Fi fast/reliable?

Allow tents?

Scenery:

Weather:

Roads: Paved   Gravel   Dirt

Site Size: Small Medium Large

Parking notes:

Overall Noise Rating: Quiet Light
Road Noise Loud   Train Noises
Loud Road Noise

Ratings: Google _____ Yelp _____ Trip Advisor _____ Campendium _____ Good Sam _____

Our personal rating: ★ ★ ★ ★ ★

A good memory:

A not-so-good memory:

Log # 41

Stop #_____ in State

_____

Campground:

Traveling Companions:

Site #   Reservation #

How Reservation Was Made: Reservation Notes:
        Online   Phone   (Who took it, who made it, how far in
Who recommended this place?   advance?)

Date Arrived: Date Departed:

Day of the Week: Day of the Week:

Time Arrived: Time Departed:

Address: State:

Zip Code: Telephone:

Website: GPS:

Travelled From: Mileage:

Preferred Route: Routes to Avoid:

Sites Along the Way: What Type of Campground?
                                              National Forest   State Park   Private
                                              Army Corps of Engineers   County
                                                  Beurue of Land Mgmt   Other

Rate: Rate Notes: (Discounts, extra fees?)

Deposit Amount:

Types of hookups: Water Hookups?
        Electric ___ Amps ____   Pressure Notes:
    Sewer _____ Dump Station ___

Security Attendant: Yes   No   Gate Code:
When?_____

Amenities

Showers: Hot Water   Pay Shower
Dry Area   Other _____

Restroom notes:

     Pool   Hot Tub   Lodge Room
          Game Room

     Adult Center   Restaurant
          Shuffleboard

     Pickleball   Tennis   Mini Golf

Fishing   Gym/Fitness Center

Other Amenities:

Things to Do

What to do while there:

What to do nearby:

Restaurants:

Wildlife we saw:

Nearby campgrounds to consider:

Grocery/General stores nearby:

Pets allowed?

Cell phone service: YES   NO

How many bars of service, usually?

Was the Wi-Fi fast/reliable?

Allow tents?

Scenery:

Weather:

Roads: Paved   Gravel   Dirt

Site Size: Small Medium Large

Parking notes:

Overall Noise Rating: Quiet Light
Road Noise Loud Train Noises
Loud Road Noise

Ratings: Google _____ Yelp _____ Trip Advisor _____ Campendium _____ Good Sam _____

Our personal rating: ★ ★ ★ ★ ★

A good memory:

A not-so-good memory:

Log # 42

Stop
#_____
in
State

_____

Campground: _____

Traveling Companions:

Site #   Reservation #

How Reservation Was Made: Reservation Notes:
          Online   Phone   (Who took it, who made it, how far in
Who recommended this place?   advance?)

Date Arrived: Date Departed:

Day of the Week: Day of the Week:

Time Arrived: Time Departed:

Address: State:

Zip Code: Telephone:

Website: GPS:

Travelled From: Mileage:

Preferred Route: Routes to Avoid:

Sites Along the Way: What Type of Campground?
                                                   National Forest   State Park   Private
                                                   Army Corps of Engineers   County
                                                      Beurue of Land Mgmt   Other

Rate: Rate Notes: (Discounts, extra fees?)

Deposit Amount:

Types of hookups: Water Hookups?
          Electric ____ Amps ____   Pressure Notes:
     Sewer _____ Dump Station ___

Security Attendant: Yes   No   Gate Code:
When?_____

Amenities

Showers: Hot Water   Pay Shower
Dry Area   Other _____

   Pool   Hot Tub   Lodge Room
        Game Room

   Pickleball   Tennis   Mini Golf

Other Amenities:

Restroom notes:

   Adult Center   Restaurant
      Shuffleboard

Fishing   Gym/Fitness Center

Things to Do

What to do while there:

What to do nearby:

Restaurants:

Wildlife we saw:

Nearby campgrounds to consider:

Grocery/General stores nearby:

Pets allowed?

Cell phone service: YES   NO

How many bars of service, usually?

Was the Wi-Fi fast/reliable?

Allow tents?

Scenery:

Weather:

Roads: Paved   Gravel   Dirt

Site Size: Small Medium Large

Parking notes:

Overall Noise Rating: Quiet Light
Road Noise Loud   Train Noises
Loud Road Noise

Ratings: Google _____ Yelp _____ Trip Advisor _____ Campendium _____ Good Sam _____

Our personal rating: ★ ★ ★ ★ ★

A good memory:

A not-so-good memory:

Log # 43

Stop #_____
in
State
_____

Campground: _____

Traveling Companions:

Site #   Reservation #

How Reservation Was Made: Reservation Notes:
          Online   Phone   (Who took it, who made it, how far in
Who recommended this place?   advance?)

Date Arrived: Date Departed:

Day of the Week: Day of the Week:

Time Arrived: Time Departed:

Address: State:

Zip Code: Telephone:

Website: GPS:

Travelled From: Mileage:

Preferred Route: Routes to Avoid:

Sites Along the Way: What Type of Campground?
                                             National Forest   State Park   Private
                                             Army Corps of Engineers   County
                                                Beurue of Land Mgmt   Other

Rate: Rate Notes: (Discounts, extra fees?)

Deposit Amount:

Types of hookups: Water Hookups?
        Electric ____ Amps ____   Pressure Notes:
     Sewer _____ Dump Station ___

Security Attendant: Yes   No   Gate Code:
When?_____

Amenities

Showers: Hot Water   Pay Shower
Dry Area   Other _____

Restroom notes:

Pool   Hot Tub   Lodge Room
Game Room

Adult Center   Restaurant
Shuffleboard

Pickleball   Tennis   Mini Golf

Fishing   Gym/Fitness Center

Other Amenities:

Things to Do

What to do while there:

What to do nearby:

Restaurants:

Wildlife we saw:

Nearby campgrounds to consider:

Grocery/General stores nearby:

Pets allowed?

Cell phone service: YES   NO

How many bars of service, usually?

Was the Wi-Fi fast/reliable?

Allow tents?

Scenery:

Weather:

Roads: Paved   Gravel   Dirt

Site Size: Small Medium Large

Parking notes:

Overall Noise Rating: Quiet Light
Road Noise Loud   Train Noises
Loud Road Noise

Ratings: Google _____ Yelp _____ Trip Advisor _____ Campendium _____ Good Sam _____

Our personal rating: ★ ★ ★ ★ ★

A good memory:

A not-so-good memory:

Log # 44

Stop #_____
in
State

_____

Campground:

Traveling Companions:

Site #

How Reservation Was Made:

      Online   Phone

Who recommended this place?

Reservation #

Reservation Notes:

(Who took it, who made it, how far in advance?)

Date Arrived:

Day of the Week:

Time Arrived:

Address:

Zip Code:

Website:

Travelled From:

Preferred Route:

Date Departed:

Day of the Week:

Time Departed:

State:

Telephone:

GPS:

Mileage:

Routes to Avoid:

Sites Along the Way:

What Type of Campground?

   National Forest State Park Private

    Army Corps of Engineers County

      Beurue of Land Mgmt Other

Rate:

Deposit Amount:

Types of hookups:

    Electric ____ Amps ____

  Sewer _____ Dump Station ____

Security Attendant: Yes No

When?_____

Rate Notes: (Discounts, extra fees?)

Water Hookups?

Pressure Notes:

Gate Code:

Amenities

Showers: Hot Water   Pay Shower
Dry Area   Other _____

   Pool   Hot Tub   Lodge Room
       Game Room

   Pickleball   Tennis   Mini Golf

Other Amenities:

Restroom notes:

   Adult Center   Restaurant
      Shuffleboard

  Fishing   Gym/Fitness Center

Things to Do

What to do while there:

What to do nearby:

Restaurants:

Wildlife we saw:

Nearby campgrounds to consider:

Grocery/General stores nearby:

Pets allowed?

Cell phone service: YES   NO

How many bars of service, usually?

Was the Wi-Fi fast/reliable?

Allow tents?

Scenery:

Weather:

Roads: Paved   Gravel   Dirt

Site Size: Small Medium Large

Parking notes:

Overall Noise Rating: Quiet Light
Road Noise Loud   Train Noises
Loud Road Noise

Ratings: Google _____ Yelp _____ Trip Advisor _____ Campendium _____ Good Sam _____

Our personal rating: ★ ★ ★ ★ ★

A good memory:

A not-so-good memory:

Log # 45

Stop #_____ in State

_____

Campground:

Traveling Companions:

Site #

How Reservation Was Made:

      Online   Phone

Who recommended this place?

Reservation #

Reservation Notes:

(Who took it, who made it, how far in advance?)

Date Arrived:

Day of the Week:

Time Arrived:

Address:

Zip Code:

Website:

Travelled From:

Preferred Route:

Date Departed:

Day of the Week:

Time Departed:

State:

Telephone:

GPS:

Mileage:

Routes to Avoid:

Sites Along the Way:

What Type of Campground?

   National Forest State Park Private

   Army Corps of Engineers County

   Beurue of Land Mgmt Other

Rate:

Deposit Amount:

Types of hookups:

    Electric ___ Amps ____

  Sewer _____ Dump Station ___

Security Attendant: Yes No

When?_____

Rate Notes: (Discounts, extra fees?)

Water Hookups?

Pressure Notes:

Gate Code:

Amenities

Showers: Hot Water   Pay Shower
Dry Area   Other _____

    Pool   Hot Tub   Lodge Room
        Game Room

    Pickleball   Tennis   Mini Golf

Other Amenities:

Restroom notes:

    Adult Center   Restaurant
        Shuffleboard

Fishing   Gym/Fitness Center

Things to Do

What to do while there:

What to do nearby:

Restaurants:

Wildlife we saw:

Nearby campgrounds to consider:

Grocery/General stores nearby:

Pets allowed?

Cell phone service: YES   NO

How many bars of service, usually?

Was the Wi-Fi fast/reliable?

Allow tents?

Scenery:

Weather:

Roads: Paved   Gravel   Dirt

Site Size: Small Medium Large

Parking notes:

Overall Noise Rating: Quiet Light
Road Noise Loud Train Noises
Loud Road Noise

Ratings: Google _____   Yelp _____   Trip Advisor _____   Campendium _____   Good Sam _____

Our personal rating: ★ ★ ★ ★ ★

A good memory:

A not-so-good memory:

Log # 46

Stop #_____
in
State

_____

Campground:

Traveling Companions:

Site #

How Reservation Was Made:
        Online   Phone

Who recommended this place?

Reservation #

Reservation Notes:
(Who took it, who made it, how far in advance?)

Date Arrived:

Day of the Week:

Time Arrived:

Address:

Zip Code:

Website:

Travelled From:

Preferred Route:

Date Departed:

Day of the Week:

Time Departed:

State:

Telephone:

GPS:

Mileage:

Routes to Avoid:

Sites Along the Way:

What Type of Campground?
    National Forest   State Park   Private
        Army Corps of Engineers   County
            Beurue of Land Mgmt   Other

Rate:

Deposit Amount:

Types of hookups:
        Electric ___ Amps ____
    Sewer _____ Dump Station ___

Security Attendant: Yes   No
When?_____

Rate Notes: (Discounts, extra fees?)

Water Hookups?

Pressure Notes:

Gate Code:

Amenities

Showers: Hot Water   Pay Shower
Dry Area   Other _____

Restroom notes:

Pool   Hot Tub   Lodge Room
Game Room

Adult Center   Restaurant
Shuffleboard

Pickleball   Tennis   Mini Golf

Fishing   Gym/Fitness Center

Other Amenities:

Things to Do

What to do while there:

What to do nearby:

Restaurants:

Wildlife we saw:

Nearby campgrounds to consider:

Grocery/General stores nearby:

Pets allowed?

Cell phone service: YES   NO

How many bars of service, usually?

Was the Wi-Fi fast/reliable?

Allow tents?

Scenery:

Weather:

Roads: Paved   Gravel   Dirt

Site Size: Small   Medium   Large

Parking notes:

Overall Noise Rating: Quiet   Light
Road Noise   Loud   Train Noises
Loud Road Noise

Ratings: Google _____ Yelp _____ Trip Advisor _____ Campendium _____ Good Sam _____

Our personal rating: ★ ★ ★ ★ ★

A good memory:

A not-so-good memory:

Log # 47

Stop #_____ **in State**

_____

Campground:

Traveling Companions:

Site #

How Reservation Was Made:
　　　Online　Phone

Who recommended this place?

Reservation #

Reservation Notes:
(Who took it, who made it, how far in advance?)

Date Arrived:

Day of the Week:

Time Arrived:

Address:

Zip Code:

Website:

Travelled From:

Preferred Route:

Date Departed:

Day of the Week:

Time Departed:

State:

Telephone:

GPS:

Mileage:

Routes to Avoid:

Sites Along the Way:

What Type of Campground?
　　National Forest　State Park　Private
　　Army Corps of Engineers　County
　　　Beurue of Land Mgmt　Other

Rate:

Deposit Amount:

Types of hookups:
　　　Electric ___ Amps ____

　Sewer _____ Dump Station ___

Security Attendant: Yes　No
When?_____

Rate Notes: (Discounts, extra fees?)

Water Hookups?

Pressure Notes:

Gate Code:

Amenities

Showers: Hot Water   Pay Shower
Dry Area   Other _____

Restroom notes:

Pool   Hot Tub   Lodge Room
Game Room

Adult Center   Restaurant
Shuffleboard

Pickleball   Tennis   Mini Golf

Fishing   Gym/Fitness Center

Other Amenities:

Things to Do

What to do while there:

What to do nearby:

Restaurants:

Wildlife we saw:

Nearby campgrounds to consider:

Grocery/General stores nearby:

Pets allowed?

Cell phone service: YES   NO

How many bars of service, usually?

Was the Wi-Fi fast/reliable?

Allow tents?

Scenery:

Weather:

Roads: Paved   Gravel   Dirt

Site Size: Small Medium Large

Parking notes:

Overall Noise Rating: Quiet Light
Road Noise Loud   Train Noises
Loud Road Noise

Ratings: Google _____ Yelp _____ Trip Advisor _____ Campendium _____ Good Sam _____

Our personal rating: ★ ★ ★ ★ ★

A good memory:

A not-so-good memory:

Log # 48

Stop #_____
in State

_____

Campground:

Traveling Companions:

Site #   Reservation #

How Reservation Was Made: Reservation Notes:
      Online   Phone   (Who took it, who made it, how far in
Who recommended this place?   advance?)

Date Arrived: Date Departed:
Day of the Week: Day of the Week:
Time Arrived: Time Departed:
Address: State:
Zip Code: Telephone:
Website: GPS:
Travelled From: Mileage:
Preferred Route: Routes to Avoid:

Sites Along the Way: What Type of Campground?
    National Forest State Park Private
    Army Corps of Engineers County
    Beurue of Land Mgmt Other

Rate: Rate Notes: (Discounts, extra fees?)
Deposit Amount:
Types of hookups: Water Hookups?
    Electric ___ Amps ___   Pressure Notes:
  Sewer _____ Dump Station ___
Security Attendant: Yes No   Gate Code:
When?_____

Amenities

Showers: Hot Water   Pay Shower
Dry Area   Other _____

    Pool   Hot Tub   Lodge Room
          Game Room

    Pickleball   Tennis   Mini Golf

Other Amenities:

Restroom notes:

    Adult Center   Restaurant
          Shuffleboard

Fishing   Gym/Fitness Center

Things to Do

What to do while there:

What to do nearby:

Restaurants:

Wildlife we saw:

Nearby campgrounds to consider:

Grocery/General stores nearby:

Pets allowed?

Cell phone service: YES   NO

How many bars of service, usually?

Was the Wi-Fi fast/reliable?

Allow tents?

Scenery:

Weather:

Roads: Paved   Gravel   Dirt

Site Size: Small Medium Large

Parking notes:

Overall Noise Rating: Quiet Light
Road Noise Loud   Train Noises
Loud Road Noise

Ratings: Google _____   Yelp _____ Trip Advisor _____   Campendium _____   Good Sam _____

Our personal rating: ★ ★ ★ ★ ★

A good memory:

A not-so-good memory:

Log # 49

**Stop
#_____
in
State**

_____

Campground: _____

Traveling Companions:

Site #

How Reservation Was Made:

      Online   Phone

Who recommended this place?

Reservation #

Reservation Notes:

(Who took it, who made it, how far in advance?)

Date Arrived:

Day of the Week:

Time Arrived:

Address:

Zip Code:

Website:

Travelled From:

Preferred Route:

Date Departed:

Day of the Week:

Time Departed:

State:

Telephone:

GPS:

Mileage:

Routes to Avoid:

Sites Along the Way:

What Type of Campground?

  National Forest State Park Private

    Army Corps of Engineers County

      Beurue of Land Mgmt Other

Rate:

Deposit Amount:

Types of hookups:

    Electric ____ Amps ____

  Sewer _____ Dump Station ____

Security Attendant: Yes No

When?_____

Rate Notes: (Discounts, extra fees?)

Water Hookups?

Pressure Notes:

Gate Code:

Amenities

Showers: Hot Water   Pay Shower
Dry Area   Other _____

Restroom notes:

Pool   Hot Tub   Lodge Room
Game Room

Adult Center   Restaurant
Shuffleboard

Pickleball   Tennis   Mini Golf

Fishing   Gym/Fitness Center

Other Amenities:

Things to Do

What to do while there:

What to do nearby:

Restaurants:

Wildlife we saw:

Nearby campgrounds to consider:

Grocery/General stores nearby:

Pets allowed?

Cell phone service: YES   NO

How many bars of service, usually?

Was the Wi-Fi fast/reliable?

Allow tents?

Scenery:

Weather:

Roads: Paved   Gravel   Dirt

Site Size: Small Medium Large

Parking notes:

Overall Noise Rating: Quiet Light
Road Noise Loud Train Noises
Loud Road Noise

Ratings: Google _____ Yelp _____ Trip Advisor _____ Campendium _____ Good Sam _____

Our personal rating: ⭐ ⭐ ⭐ ⭐ ⭐

A good memory:

A not-so-good memory:

Log # 50

Stop #_____
in
State

_____

Campground: _____

Traveling Companions:

Site #   Reservation #

How Reservation Was Made: Reservation Notes:
          Online   Phone   (Who took it, who made it, how far in
Who recommended this place?   advance?)

Date Arrived: Date Departed:

Day of the Week: Day of the Week:

Time Arrived: Time Departed:

Address: State:

Zip Code: Telephone:

Website: GPS:

Travelled From: Mileage:

Preferred Route: Routes to Avoid:

Sites Along the Way: What Type of Campground?
                                             National Forest   State Park   Private
                                             Army Corps of Engineers   County
                                                Beurue of Land Mgmt   Other

Rate: Rate Notes: (Discounts, extra fees?)

Deposit Amount:

Types of hookups: Water Hookups?
         Electric ___ Amps ____   Pressure Notes:
      Sewer _____ Dump Station ___

Security Attendant: Yes   No   Gate Code:
When?_____

Amenities

Showers: Hot Water   Pay Shower
Dry Area   Other _____

Pool   Hot Tub   Lodge Room
Game Room

Pickleball   Tennis   Mini Golf

Other Amenities:

Restroom notes:

Adult Center   Restaurant
Shuffleboard

Fishing   Gym/Fitness Center

Things to Do

What to do while there:

What to do nearby:

Restaurants:

Wildlife we saw:

Nearby campgrounds to consider:

Grocery/General stores nearby:

Pets allowed?

Cell phone service: YES   NO

How many bars of service, usually?

Was the Wi-Fi fast/reliable?

Allow tents?

Scenery:

Weather:

Roads: Paved   Gravel   Dirt

Site Size: Small Medium Large

Parking notes:

Overall Noise Rating: Quiet Light
Road Noise Loud   Train Noises
Loud Road Noise

Ratings: Google _____ Yelp _____ Trip Advisor _____ Campendium _____ Good Sam _____

Our personal rating: ★ ★ ★ ★ ★

A good memory:

A not-so-good memory:

Part 2: Maintenance Logs

Use the tables in this section to keep track of your RV/Camper maintenance. In each table, take note of the pertinent information for your records. This way, you will have a quick log of what you have done to keep your RV working reliably.

Make   Model   Extras

Date: Mileage:

Service: Who completed the service:

Date: Mileage:

Service: Who completed the service:

Date: Mileage:

Service: Who completed the service:

Date: Mileage:

Service: Who completed the service:

Date: Mileage:

Service: Who completed the service:

Date: Mileage:

Service: Who completed the service:

Date: Mileage:

Service: Who completed the service:

Date: Mileage:

Service: Who completed the service:

Date: Mileage:

Service: Who completed the service:

Date: Mileage:

Service: Who completed the service:

Date: Mileage:

Service: Who completed the service:

Date: Mileage:

Service: Who completed the service:

Date: Mileage:

Service: Who completed the service:

Date: Mileage:

Service: Who completed the service:

Date: Mileage:

Service: Who completed the service:

Date: Mileage:

Service: Who completed the service:

Date: Mileage:

Service: Who completed the service:

Date: Mileage:

Service: Who completed the service:

Date: Mileage:

Service: Who completed the service:

Date: Mileage:

Service: Who completed the service:

Date: Mileage:

Service: Who completed the service:

Date: Mileage:

Service: Who completed the service:

Date: Mileage:

Service: Who completed the service:

Date: Mileage:

Service: Who completed the service:

Part 3: Supply Lists

A prepared camper is a happy camper!

Some supplies you will keep with you all the time, but some trips require special planning as far as supplies go.

Use this section to keep track of the basics as well as those unusual special supplies you need on your adventures.

The suggested supplies checklist is just that – a suggestion. Maybe it will help you remember the absolute essentials.

Trip to:

Date:

The essentials (checklist)

Surge protector	Electrical adaptors	Toilet chemicals
Sewer kit	RV-friendly toilet paper	Water pressure valve
Drinking water hose	Leveling blocks	Tire pressure gauge
Extension cords	Wheel chocks	Shovel
Eletrical tape	Duct tape	Extra cotter pins
Extra motor oil	Extra transmission fluid	Flashlight
Jumper cables	Emergency road kit	Fire extinguisher
Driver license	Vehicle registrations	Vehicle insurance cards
Medical insurance cards	First aid kit	Medications
Sunscreen	Bug Spray	Batteries
Campground directory	Soap/Shampoo	Toothpaste/brush
Camera	Camping chairs	Sheets/Blankets
Towels	Rain Gear	Sewing kit

Other Supplies

Trip to:

Date:

The essentials (checklist)

Surge protector	Electrical adaptors	Toilet chemicals
Sewer kit	RV-friendly toilet paper	Water pressure valve
Drinking water hose	Leveling blocks	Tire pressure gauge
Extension cords	Wheel chocks	Shovel
Eletrical tape	Duct tape	Extra cotter pins
Extra motor oil	Extra transmission fluid	Flashlight
Jumper cables	Emergency road kit	Fire extinguisher
Driver license	Vehicle registrations	Vehicle insurance cards
Medical insurance cards	First aid kit	Medications
Sunscreen	Bug Spray	Batteries
Campground directory	Soap/Shampoo	Toothpaste/brush
Camera	Camping chairs	Sheets/Blankets
Towels	Rain Gear	Sewing kit

Other Supplies

Trip to:

Date:

The essentials (checklist)

Surge protector	Electrical adaptors	Toilet chemicals
Sewer kit	RV-friendly toilet paper	Water pressure valve
Drinking water hose	Leveling blocks	Tire pressure gauge
Extension cords	Wheel chocks	Shovel
Eletrical tape	Duct tape	Extra cotter pins
Extra motor oil	Extra transmission fluid	Flashlight
Jumper cables	Emergency road kit	Fire extinguisher
Driver license	Vehicle registrations	Vehicle insurance cards
Medical insurance cards	First aid kit	Medications
Sunscreen	Bug Spray	Batteries
Campground directory	Soap/Shampoo	Toothpaste/brush
Camera	Camping chairs	Sheets/Blankets
Towels	Rain Gear	Sewing kit

Other Supplies

Trip to:

Date:

The essentials (checklist)

Surge protector	Electrical adaptors	Toilet chemicals
Sewer kit	RV-friendly toilet paper	Water pressure valve
Drinking water hose	Leveling blocks	Tire pressure gauge
Extension cords	Wheel chocks	Shovel
Eletrical tape	Duct tape	Extra cotter pins
Extra motor oil	Extra transmission fluid	Flashlight
Jumper cables	Emergency road kit	Fire extinguisher
Driver license	Vehicle registrations	Vehicle insurance cards
Medical insurance cards	First aid kit	Medications
Sunscreen	Bug Spray	Batteries
Campground directory	Soap/Shampoo	Toothpaste/brush
Camera	Camping chairs	Sheets/Blankets
Towels	Rain Gear	Sewing kit

Other Supplies

Trip to:

Date:

The essentials (checklist)

Surge protector	Electrical adaptors	Toilet chemicals
Sewer kit	RV-friendly toilet paper	Water pressure valve
Drinking water hose	Leveling blocks	Tire pressure gauge
Extension cords	Wheel chocks	Shovel
Eletrical tape	Duct tape	Extra cotter pins
Extra motor oil	Extra transmission fluid	Flashlight
Jumper cables	Emergency road kit	Fire extinguisher
Driver license	Vehicle registrations	Vehicle insurance cards
Medical insurance cards	First aid kit	Medications
Sunscreen	Bug Spray	Batteries
Campground directory	Soap/Shampoo	Toothpaste/brush
Camera	Camping chairs	Sheets/Blankets
Towels	Rain Gear	Sewing kit

Other Supplies

Trip to:

Date:

The essentials (checklist)

Surge protector	Electrical adaptors	Toilet chemicals
Sewer kit	RV-friendly toilet paper	Water pressure valve
Drinking water hose	Leveling blocks	Tire pressure gauge
Extension cords	Wheel chocks	Shovel
Eletrical tape	Duct tape	Extra cotter pins
Extra motor oil	Extra transmission fluid	Flashlight
Jumper cables	Emergency road kit	Fire extinguisher
Driver license	Vehicle registrations	Vehicle insurance cards
Medical insurance cards	First aid kit	Medications
Sunscreen	Bug Spray	Batteries
Campground directory	Soap/Shampoo	Toothpaste/brush
Camera	Camping chairs	Sheets/Blankets
Towels	Rain Gear	Sewing kit

Other Supplies

Trip to:

Date:

The essentials (checklist)

Surge protector	Electrical adaptors	Toilet chemicals
Sewer kit	RV-friendly toilet paper	Water pressure valve
Drinking water hose	Leveling blocks	Tire pressure gauge
Extension cords	Wheel chocks	Shovel
Eletrical tape	Duct tape	Extra cotter pins
Extra motor oil	Extra transmission fluid	Flashlight
Jumper cables	Emergency road kit	Fire extinguisher
Driver license	Vehicle registrations	Vehicle insurance cards
Medical insurance cards	First aid kit	Medications
Sunscreen	Bug Spray	Batteries
Campground directory	Soap/Shampoo	Toothpaste/brush
Camera	Camping chairs	Sheets/Blankets
Towels	Rain Gear	Sewing kit

Other Supplies

Trip to:

Date:

The essentials (checklist)

Surge protector	Electrical adaptors	Toilet chemicals
Sewer kit	RV-friendly toilet paper	Water pressure valve
Drinking water hose	Leveling blocks	Tire pressure gauge
Extension cords	Wheel chocks	Shovel
Eletrical tape	Duct tape	Extra cotter pins
Extra motor oil	Extra transmission fluid	Flashlight
Jumper cables	Emergency road kit	Fire extinguisher
Driver license	Vehicle registrations	Vehicle insurance cards
Medical insurance cards	First aid kit	Medications
Sunscreen	Bug Spray	Batteries
Campground directory	Soap/Shampoo	Toothpaste/brush
Camera	Camping chairs	Sheets/Blankets
Towels	Rain Gear	Sewing kit

Other Supplies

Trip to:

Date:

The essentials (checklist)

Surge protector	Electrical adaptors	Toilet chemicals
Sewer kit	RV-friendly toilet paper	Water pressure valve
Drinking water hose	Leveling blocks	Tire pressure gauge
Extension cords	Wheel chocks	Shovel
Eletrical tape	Duct tape	Extra cotter pins
Extra motor oil	Extra transmission fluid	Flashlight
Jumper cables	Emergency road kit	Fire extinguisher
Driver license	Vehicle registrations	Vehicle insurance cards
Medical insurance cards	First aid kit	Medications
Sunscreen	Bug Spray	Batteries
Campground directory	Soap/Shampoo	Toothpaste/brush
Camera	Camping chairs	Sheets/Blankets
Towels	Rain Gear	Sewing kit

Other Supplies

Trip to:

Date:

The essentials (checklist)

Surge protector	Electrical adaptors	Toilet chemicals
Sewer kit	RV-friendly toilet paper	Water pressure valve
Drinking water hose	Leveling blocks	Tire pressure gauge
Extension cords	Wheel chocks	Shovel
Eletrical tape	Duct tape	Extra cotter pins
Extra motor oil	Extra transmission fluid	Flashlight
Jumper cables	Emergency road kit	Fire extinguisher
Driver license	Vehicle registrations	Vehicle insurance cards
Medical insurance cards	First aid kit	Medications
Sunscreen	Bug Spray	Batteries
Campground directory	Soap/Shampoo	Toothpaste/brush
Camera	Camping chairs	Sheets/Blankets
Towels	Rain Gear	Sewing kit

Other Supplies

Trip to:

Date:

The essentials (checklist)

Surge protector	Electrical adaptors	Toilet chemicals
Sewer kit	RV-friendly toilet paper	Water pressure valve
Drinking water hose	Leveling blocks	Tire pressure gauge
Extension cords	Wheel chocks	Shovel
Eletrical tape	Duct tape	Extra cotter pins
Extra motor oil	Extra transmission fluid	Flashlight
Jumper cables	Emergency road kit	Fire extinguisher
Driver license	Vehicle registrations	Vehicle insurance cards
Medical insurance cards	First aid kit	Medications
Sunscreen	Bug Spray	Batteries
Campground directory	Soap/Shampoo	Toothpaste/brush
Camera	Camping chairs	Sheets/Blankets
Towels	Rain Gear	Sewing kit

Other Supplies

Trip to:

Date:

The essentials (checklist)

Surge protector	Electrical adaptors	Toilet chemicals
Sewer kit	RV-friendly toilet paper	Water pressure valve
Drinking water hose	Leveling blocks	Tire pressure gauge
Extension cords	Wheel chocks	Shovel
Eletrical tape	Duct tape	Extra cotter pins
Extra motor oil	Extra transmission fluid	Flashlight
Jumper cables	Emergency road kit	Fire extinguisher
Driver license	Vehicle registrations	Vehicle insurance cards
Medical insurance cards	First aid kit	Medications
Sunscreen	Bug Spray	Batteries
Campground directory	Soap/Shampoo	Toothpaste/brush
Camera	Camping chairs	Sheets/Blankets
Towels	Rain Gear	Sewing kit

Other Supplies

Trip to:

Date:

The essentials (checklist)

Surge protector	Electrical adaptors	Toilet chemicals
Sewer kit	RV-friendly toilet paper	Water pressure valve
Drinking water hose	Leveling blocks	Tire pressure gauge
Extension cords	Wheel chocks	Shovel
Eletrical tape	Duct tape	Extra cotter pins
Extra motor oil	Extra transmission fluid	Flashlight
Jumper cables	Emergency road kit	Fire extinguisher
Driver license	Vehicle registrations	Vehicle insurance cards
Medical insurance cards	First aid kit	Medications
Sunscreen	Bug Spray	Batteries
Campground directory	Soap/Shampoo	Toothpaste/brush
Camera	Camping chairs	Sheets/Blankets
Towels	Rain Gear	Sewing kit

Other Supplies

Trip to:

Date:

The essentials (checklist)

Surge protector	Electrical adaptors	Toilet chemicals
Sewer kit	RV-friendly toilet paper	Water pressure valve
Drinking water hose	Leveling blocks	Tire pressure gauge
Extension cords	Wheel chocks	Shovel
Eletrical tape	Duct tape	Extra cotter pins
Extra motor oil	Extra transmission fluid	Flashlight
Jumper cables	Emergency road kit	Fire extinguisher
Driver license	Vehicle registrations	Vehicle insurance cards
Medical insurance cards	First aid kit	Medications
Sunscreen	Bug Spray	Batteries
Campground directory	Soap/Shampoo	Toothpaste/brush
Camera	Camping chairs	Sheets/Blankets
Towels	Rain Gear	Sewing kit

Other Supplies

Trip to:

Date:

The essentials (checklist)

Surge protector	Electrical adaptors	Toilet chemicals
Sewer kit	RV-friendly toilet paper	Water pressure valve
Drinking water hose	Leveling blocks	Tire pressure gauge
Extension cords	Wheel chocks	Shovel
Eletrical tape	Duct tape	Extra cotter pins
Extra motor oil	Extra transmission fluid	Flashlight
Jumper cables	Emergency road kit	Fire extinguisher
Driver license	Vehicle registrations	Vehicle insurance cards
Medical insurance cards	First aid kit	Medications
Sunscreen	Bug Spray	Batteries
Campground directory	Soap/Shampoo	Toothpaste/brush
Camera	Camping chairs	Sheets/Blankets
Towels	Rain Gear	Sewing kit

Other Supplies

Trip to:

Date:

The essentials (checklist)

Surge protector	Electrical adaptors	Toilet chemicals
Sewer kit	RV-friendly toilet paper	Water pressure valve
Drinking water hose	Leveling blocks	Tire pressure gauge
Extension cords	Wheel chocks	Shovel
Eletrical tape	Duct tape	Extra cotter pins
Extra motor oil	Extra transmission fluid	Flashlight
Jumper cables	Emergency road kit	Fire extinguisher
Driver license	Vehicle registrations	Vehicle insurance cards
Medical insurance cards	First aid kit	Medications
Sunscreen	Bug Spray	Batteries
Campground directory	Soap/Shampoo	Toothpaste/brush
Camera	Camping chairs	Sheets/Blankets
Towels	Rain Gear	Sewing kit

Other Supplies

Trip to:

Date:

The essentials (checklist)

Surge protector	Electrical adaptors	Toilet chemicals
Sewer kit	RV-friendly toilet paper	Water pressure valve
Drinking water hose	Leveling blocks	Tire pressure gauge
Extension cords	Wheel chocks	Shovel
Eletrical tape	Duct tape	Extra cotter pins
Extra motor oil	Extra transmission fluid	Flashlight
Jumper cables	Emergency road kit	Fire extinguisher
Driver license	Vehicle registrations	Vehicle insurance cards
Medical insurance cards	First aid kit	Medications
Sunscreen	Bug Spray	Batteries
Campground directory	Soap/Shampoo	Toothpaste/brush
Camera	Camping chairs	Sheets/Blankets
Towels	Rain Gear	Sewing kit

Other Supplies

Trip to:

Date:

The essentials (checklist)

Surge protector	Electrical adaptors	Toilet chemicals
Sewer kit	RV-friendly toilet paper	Water pressure valve
Drinking water hose	Leveling blocks	Tire pressure gauge
Extension cords	Wheel chocks	Shovel
Eletrical tape	Duct tape	Extra cotter pins
Extra motor oil	Extra transmission fluid	Flashlight
Jumper cables	Emergency road kit	Fire extinguisher
Driver license	Vehicle registrations	Vehicle insurance cards
Medical insurance cards	First aid kit	Medications
Sunscreen	Bug Spray	Batteries
Campground directory	Soap/Shampoo	Toothpaste/brush
Camera	Camping chairs	Sheets/Blankets
Towels	Rain Gear	Sewing kit

Other Supplies

Trip to:

Date:

The essentials (checklist)

Surge protector	Electrical adaptors	Toilet chemicals
Sewer kit	RV-friendly toilet paper	Water pressure valve
Drinking water hose	Leveling blocks	Tire pressure gauge
Extension cords	Wheel chocks	Shovel
Eletrical tape	Duct tape	Extra cotter pins
Extra motor oil	Extra transmission fluid	Flashlight
Jumper cables	Emergency road kit	Fire extinguisher
Driver license	Vehicle registrations	Vehicle insurance cards
Medical insurance cards	First aid kit	Medications
Sunscreen	Bug Spray	Batteries
Campground directory	Soap/Shampoo	Toothpaste/brush
Camera	Camping chairs	Sheets/Blankets
Towels	Rain Gear	Sewing kit

Other Supplies

Trip to:

Date:

The essentials (checklist)

Surge protector	Electrical adaptors	Toilet chemicals
Sewer kit	RV-friendly toilet paper	Water pressure valve
Drinking water hose	Leveling blocks	Tire pressure gauge
Extension cords	Wheel chocks	Shovel
Eletrical tape	Duct tape	Extra cotter pins
Extra motor oil	Extra transmission fluid	Flashlight
Jumper cables	Emergency road kit	Fire extinguisher
Driver license	Vehicle registrations	Vehicle insurance cards
Medical insurance cards	First aid kit	Medications
Sunscreen	Bug Spray	Batteries
Campground directory	Soap/Shampoo	Toothpaste/brush
Camera	Camping chairs	Sheets/Blankets
Towels	Rain Gear	Sewing kit

Other Supplies

Part 4: Menu Planner

A well-fed camper is a happy camper!

Finding something that everyone you're traveling with likes to eat can be a challenge, especially if you're also dealing with any kind of food allergy.

When you're in a small kitchen like your RV or fireside camp, you don't have the usual luxuries of a full-sized kitchen.

This menu planner will help you determine what ingredients, utensils, and pans to pack for your adventure.

Week of:

Destination:

	Breakfast	Lunch	Dinner	Snacks
Sunday				
Monday				
Tuesday				
Wednesday				
Thursday				
Friday				
Saturday				

Week of:

Destination:

	Breakfast	Lunch	Dinner	Snacks
Sunday				
Monday				
Tuesday				
Wednesday				
Thursday				
Friday				
Saturday				

Week of:

Destination:

	Breakfast	Lunch	Dinner	Snacks
Sunday				
Monday				
Tuesday				
Wednesday				
Thursday				
Friday				
Saturday				

Week of:

Destination:

	Breakfast	Lunch	Dinner	Snacks
Sunday				
Monday				
Tuesday				
Wednesday				
Thursday				
Friday				
Saturday				

Week of:

Destination:

	Breakfast	Lunch	Dinner	Snacks
Sunday				
Monday				
Tuesday				
Wednesday				
Thursday				
Friday				
Saturday				

Week of:

Destination:

	Breakfast	Lunch	Dinner	Snacks
Sunday				
Monday				
Tuesday				
Wednesday				
Thursday				
Friday				
Saturday				

Week of:

Destination:

	Breakfast	Lunch	Dinner	Snacks
Sunday				
Monday				
Tuesday				
Wednesday				
Thursday				
Friday				
Saturday				

Week of:

Destination:

	Breakfast	Lunch	Dinner	Snacks
Sunday				
Monday				
Tuesday				
Wednesday				
Thursday				
Friday				
Saturday				

Week of:

Destination:

	Breakfast	Lunch	Dinner	Snacks
Sunday				
Monday				
Tuesday				
Wednesday				
Thursday				
Friday				
Saturday				

Week of:

Destination:

	Breakfast	Lunch	Dinner	Snacks
Sunday				
Monday				
Tuesday				
Wednesday				
Thursday				
Friday				
Saturday				

Week of:

Destination:

	Breakfast	Lunch	Dinner	Snacks
Sunday				
Monday				
Tuesday				
Wednesday				
Thursday				
Friday				
Saturday				

Week of:

Destination:

	Breakfast	Lunch	Dinner	Snacks
Sunday				
Monday				
Tuesday				
Wednesday				
Thursday				
Friday				
Saturday				

Week of:

Destination:

	Breakfast	Lunch	Dinner	Snacks
Sunday				
Monday				
Tuesday				
Wednesday				
Thursday				
Friday				
Saturday				

Week of:

Destination:

	Breakfast	Lunch	Dinner	Snacks
Sunday				
Monday				
Tuesday				
Wednesday				
Thursday				
Friday				
Saturday				

Week of:

Destination:

	Breakfast	Lunch	Dinner	Snacks
Sunday				
Monday				
Tuesday				
Wednesday				
Thursday				
Friday				
Saturday				

Week of:

Destination:

	Breakfast	Lunch	Dinner	Snacks
Sunday				
Monday				
Tuesday				
Wednesday				
Thursday				
Friday				
Saturday				

Week of:

Destination:

	Breakfast	Lunch	Dinner	Snacks
Sunday				
Monday				
Tuesday				
Wednesday				
Thursday				
Friday				
Saturday				

Week of:

Destination:

	Breakfast	Lunch	Dinner	Snacks
Sunday				
Monday				
Tuesday				
Wednesday				
Thursday				
Friday				
Saturday				

Week of:

Destination:

	Breakfast	Lunch	Dinner	Snacks
Sunday				
Monday				
Tuesday				
Wednesday				
Thursday				
Friday				
Saturday				

Week of:

Destination:

	Breakfast	Lunch	Dinner	Snacks
Sunday				
Monday				
Tuesday				
Wednesday				
Thursday				
Friday				
Saturday				

Week of:

Destination:

	Breakfast	Lunch	Dinner	Snacks
Sunday				
Monday				
Tuesday				
Wednesday				
Thursday				
Friday				
Saturday				

Week of:

Destination:

	Breakfast	Lunch	Dinner	Snacks
Sunday				
Monday				
Tuesday				
Wednesday				
Thursday				
Friday				
Saturday				

Week of:

Destination:

	Breakfast	Lunch	Dinner	Snacks
Sunday				
Monday				
Tuesday				
Wednesday				
Thursday				
Friday				
Saturday				

Week of:

Destination:

	Breakfast	Lunch	Dinner	Snacks
Sunday				
Monday				
Tuesday				
Wednesday				
Thursday				
Friday				
Saturday				

Week of:

Destination:

	Breakfast	Lunch	Dinner	Snacks
Sunday				
Monday				
Tuesday				
Wednesday				
Thursday				
Friday				
Saturday				

Week of:

Destination:

	Breakfast	Lunch	Dinner	Snacks
Sunday				
Monday				
Tuesday				
Wednesday				
Thursday				
Friday				
Saturday				

Quick Reference System

Use this quick reference system as a guide to help you find any of your log entries at a glance. This reference is organized by state, then page number, log number, and campground name.

Alabama

Page Number	Log Number	Campground Name

Arizona

Page Number	Log Number	Campground Name

Arkansas

Page Number	Log Number	Campground Name

California

Page Number	Log Number	Campground Name

Colorado

Page Number	Log Number	Campground Name

Connecticut

Page Number	Log Number	Campground Name

Delaware

Page Number	Log Number	Campground Name

Florida

Page Number	Log Number	Campground Name

Georgia

Page Number	Log Number	Campground Name

Idaho

Page Number	Log Number	Campground Name

Illinois

Page Number	Log Number	Campground Name

Indiana

Page Number	Log Number	Campground Name

Iowa

Page Number	Log Number	Campground Name

Kansas

Page Number	Log Number	Campground Name

Kentucky

Page Number	Log Number	Campground Name

Lousiana

Page Number	Log Number	Campground Name

Maine

Page Number	Log Number	Campground Name

Maryland

Page Number	Log Number	Campground Name

Massachusetts

Page Number	Log Number	Campground Name

Michigan

Page Number	Log Number	Campground Name

Minnesota

Page Number	Log Number	Campground Name

Mississippi

Page Number	Log Number	Campground Name

Missouri

Page Number	Log Number	Campground Name

Montana

Page Number	Log Number	Campground Name

Nebraska

Page Number	Log Number	Campground Name

Nevada

Page Number	Log Number	Campground Name

New Hampshire

Page Number	Log Number	Campground Name

New Jersey

Page Number	Log Number	Campground Name

New Mexico

Page Number	Log Number	Campground Name

New York

Page Number	Log Number	Campground Name

North Carolina

Page Number	Log Number	Campground Name

North Dakota

Page Number	Log Number	Campground Name

Ohio

Page Number	Log Number	Campground Name

Oklahoma

Page Number	Log Number	Campground Name

Oregon

Page Number	Log Number	Campground Name

Pennsylvania

Page Number	Log Number	Campground Name

Rhode Island

Page Number	Log Number	Campground Name

South Carolina

Page Number	Log Number	Campground Name

South Dakota

Page Number	Log Number	Campground Name

Tennessee

Page Number	Log Number	Campground Name

Page Number	Log Number	Campground Name

Utah

Page Number	Log Number	Campground Name

Vermont

Page Number	Log Number	Campground Name

Virginia

Page Number	Log Number	Campground Name

Washington

Page Number	Log Number	Campground Name

West Virginia

Page Number	Log Number	Campground Name

Wisconsin

Page Number	Log Number	Campground Name

Wyoming

Page Number	Log Number	Campground Name

Notes: